ESSENTIAL CANADA WEST

★ Best places to see 34–55

■ Featured sight

Original text by Karen Pieringer and Fiona Malins
Updated by Des Hannigan

First published 2007
Revised 2009

Series Editor Karen Kemp
Series Designer Sharon Rudd
Cartographic Editor Anna Thompson

ISBN: 978-0-7495-6123-9

Published by AA Publishing, a trading name of AA Media Limited, whose registered office is Fanum House, Basing View, Basingstoke, Hampshire RG21 4EA. Registered number 06112600.

A CIP catalogue record for this book is available from the British Library

Colour separation: MRM Graphics Ltd
Printed and bound in Italy by Printer Trento S.r.l.

A03804
Maps in this title produced from map data © Tele Atlas N.V. 2005 Tele Atlas

About this book

Symbols are used to denote the following categories:

- map reference to maps on cover
- address or location
- telephone number
- opening times
- admission charge
- restaurant or café on premises or nearby
- nearest underground train station
- nearest bus/tram route
- nearest overground train station
- nearest ferry stop
- nearest airport
- tourist information
- other practical information
- ➤ indicates the page where you will find a fuller description

This book is divided into five sections.

The essence of Western Canada pages 6–19
Introduction; Features; Food and drink; Short break including the 10 Essentials

Planning pages 20–33
Before you go; Getting there; Getting around; Being there

Best places to see pages 34–55
The unmissable highlights of any visit to Western Canada

Best things to do pages 56–73
Great places to have lunch; top activities; stunning views

Exploring pages 74–186
The best places to visit in Western Canada, organized by area

♦ to ♦♦♦♦♦ denotes AAA rating

Maps

All map references are to the maps on the covers. For example, Banff has the reference 17L – indicating the grid square in which it is to be found.

Admission prices

Inexpensive (under $5)
Moderate ($5–$8)
Expensive (over $8)

Hotel prices

Per room per night:
$ budget (under $100);
$$ moderate ($100–$200);
$$$ expensive ($201–$300);
$$$$ luxury (over $300)

Restaurant prices

3-course meal per person without drinks:
$ budget (under $25);
$$ moderate ($25–$50);
$$$ expensive (over $50)

Contents

The essence of...

Western Canada extends for over 1,770km (1,100 miles) from Winnipeg to the Pacific coast of British Columbia. North to south it measures over 2,895km (1,800 miles) from Baffin Island to the US border. This is big country in every sense. The choices facing you are fascinating – the spectacular glaciers, lakes and forests of the Rocky Mountains, the deep inlets and islands of the British Columbia seaboard, the farmlands and Old West culture of the Prairies and the enthralling wildlife of the northern wilderness. Western Canada also has vibrant and colorful urban centers such as Vancouver, Victoria, Calgary, Edmonton and Winnipeg.

features

Western Canada is an enthralling world of wide-open spaces. Some may claim that the Prairies are monotonous, but they are an exhilarating part of the westward journey towards the Rocky Mountains through vibrant landscapes of golden wheat, blue flowered flax and yellow rape fields beneath vast skies.

Beyond Calgary the mountains loom large on the horizon. Soon, you cross into British Columbia – "Beautiful BC" or "Super, Natural BC," as its proud residents call it in justifiable acknowledgement of some of the world's most spectacular mountain and coastal scenery. The region's great cities of Vancouver and Victoria sit in modern urban splendor amidst it all.

Northern Canada is awe-inspiring, a world that enjoys 24 hours of summer daylight to balance its winter darkness. Here, the majestic Mackenzie River flows to the icy Beaufort Sea, mountainous Baffin Island straddles the Arctic Circle and the Yukon draws you into a wilderness of stunning landscapes.

GEOGRAPHY

- Population: 9.5 million.
- Greatest river: Mackenzie (1,800km/1,118 miles).
- Biggest lakes: Great Bear (31,328sq km/

12,100sq miles), Great Slave (28,568sq km/ 11,034sq miles), and Lake Winnipeg (23,750sq km/ 9,170sq miles). Great Slave is the deepest (614m/2,014ft).

- Highest peak: Mount Logan (5,950m/19,520ft).
- The Arctic archipelago is the largest group of islands in the world. The biggest is Baffin (➤ 175) at 507,451sq km (195,875sq miles).

FAMOUS PRODUCTS

- The West Coast First Nations are renowned for woodcarving and making jewelry and other items.
- Pacific salmon, caught offshore and in the rivers, are delicious, especially when smoked.
- The Okanagan Valley in BC is famous for fruit orchards and wineries (➤ 99).
- Alberta beef, grazed on prairie meadows, is supremely succulent.
- The Inuit people of Arctic Canada produce evocative artworks, including carvings, lithographs and etchings.
- Yukon jewelers use local gold to create beautiful pieces.

WILDLIFE

- The Western mountain ranges are home to moose, elk, deer, black and grizzly bears and sheep.
- Bison (North American buffalo) only roam freely within the Wood Buffalo National Park, but can also be viewed in paddocks at Elk Island, Prince Albert and Waterton Lakes (➤ 100).
- Off the coast, pods of migrating whales are often seen, along with the resident populations of orcas, seals, other sea mammals and a variety of birds.
- The bald eagle population of BC is over 25,000 and may be much more, with huge numbers at Brackendale in winter.

food & drink

Some of the best ingredients in Canada are found in the west, from Pacific and Arctic seafood to Alberta beef and the fruits and wines of the Okanagan Valley. In the top city restaurants they are used in exciting fusion cuisine.

FIRST NATIONS FOOD

Even before the first Europeans arrived in the mid-19th century, bringing their cattle with them, protein in all its fleshy forms dominated the diets of the First Nations tribes who wandered across the region in search of food. They caught fish, of course – trout, grayling, char, muskellunge (a type of pike), sturgeon and whitefish, primarily from the lakes in Manitoba and northern Saskatchewan. But most of them depended for survival on the huge herds of bison that roamed the Prairies.

Elements of the aboriginal diet can still be found on the Prairies. Bison burgers and bison steaks are

still available, although most of the bison meat served today comes from farm-raised animals.

PRAIRIES SPECIALTIES

The main source of protein these days is beef, and Alberta's ranches produce some of the best in the world – juicy, marbled and ready for the grill – and the West is for the most part unapologetic about its carnivorous appetites.

Successive waves of immigrants have added their flavors to this meat-and-potatoes landscape. Ukrainians brought borscht, cabbage rolls and *pirogis* (little boiled dumplings stuffed with potatoes or cheese or vegetables); and Mennonite farmers from Germany adapted the sausages of home to local tastes, often by switching the emphasis from pork to beef.

SEAFOOD AND FRESHWATER FISH

Across the mountains, the whole culinary picture changes dramatically. What beef is to the Prairies, salmon is to British Columbia, and the region's chefs – heavily influenced by the new-wave cooking of California and Washington state across the border – serve filets glazed with Asian spices or raw as sushi or poached with pineapples. But one of the most popular ways to prepare it remains to

cook it as the Pacific First Nations did – barbecued on a soaked cedar plank. The West Coast fisheries provide more than just salmon, of course. Fresh sole, halibut, Alaskan king crab and its Dungeness cousin, Fanny Bay oysters, clams and ling cod are among the bounty that appear regularly on local menus and in local markets.

North of 60 in Yukon, the Northwest Territories and Nunavut, the range of local delicacies narrows considerably, but the fish is marvelous. Trout from cold mountain lakes are particularly sweet and a well-cooked and fresh Arctic char makes salmon taste almost pedestrian by comparison.

DRINK

Traditionally, beer and whiskey were the thirst-quenchers of Canadians, and today domestic beers such as Labatt Blue and Molson Canadian dominate, although regional favorites such as Kokanee lager from British Columbia's Kootenay region are hugely popular, while micro-breweries are producing increasingly appealing beers.

Canadian wine is not yet a world leader. The main producers are in Ontario, but British Columbia's Okanagan region (► 99) is building a solid reputation in viniculture with a rack of fruity, deep-tasting vintages. Canada's celebrated "ice wine," made from frozen grapes, and noted for the intensity of its flavor and texture, has some world leaders in Okanagan vintages.

short break

If you have only a short time to visit Western Canada and would like to take home some unforgettable memories you can do something local and capture the real flavor of the country. The following suggestions will give you a wide range of sights and experiences that won't take very long, won't cost very much and will make your visit very special.

- **Join in the excitement** of the chuckwagon races and the rodeo at the Calgary Stampede, or attend one of the many rodeo events in Prairies cowboy country.

- **Follow a trail** through Horseshoe Canyon near Drumheller (➤ 156), amid the stunning scenery of the Badlands of Alberta, world-famous as a dinosaur graveyard.

- **Travel west across Saskatchewan** from the Manitoba border for the full impact of the wide open spaces of the Prairies, with wheat fields stretching to the horizon beneath enormous skies that are full of stars at night.

- **Drive toward the Rockies** from Calgary, watching the wall of mountains get ever nearer as the plains dissolve beneath your wheels.

- **Walk to the base of Mount Edith Cavell** in Jasper National Park (➤ 44–45) and gaze up at the Angel Glacier, named for its two "wings" of ice.

- **Wander along the shores** of any of the famous Rocky Mountain lakes and marvel at the remarkable color of the water (➤ 50–51).

- **Sit on the beach** at sunset in Pacific Rim National Park (➤ 124–125), watching the sun disappear beyond the ocean.

- **Stay up late** on the Arctic Circle at Pangnirtung on Baffin Island (➤ 175) in late June and enjoy the midnight sun, or time your visit to see the amazing displays of the aurora borealis (Northern Lights), painting the sky with its dancing colored light.

- **Take a wildlife-spotting trip,** perhaps to view the polar bears at Churchill, Manitoba (➤ 152), on the shores of Hudson Bay, or to skim the waves amid pods of whales off the BC coast.

- **Walk the wooden boardwalks** of Dawson City (➤ 172–173), in the Yukon, and imagine the Gold-Rush fever that gripped the town more than a century ago.

Planning

Before you go

WHEN TO GO (VANCOUVER)

JAN	FEB	MAR	APR	MAY	JUN	JUL	AUG	SEP	OCT	NOV	DEC
6°C	7°C	11°C	14°C	17°C	21°C	23°C	22°C	19°C	14°C	9°C	6°C
43°F	45°F	52°F	57°F	63°F	70°F	73°F	72°F	66°F	57°F	48°F	43°F

High season · Low season

The best weather in western Canada is in July and August, with temperatures rising to above 26.5°C (80°F), but it is also the busiest time to travel. The Prairies are bitterly cold in the winter, but have beautiful warm summers, although thunderstorms can occur. Summer is the best time to visit the Rockies, but many mountain areas are busy during the winter skiing season (Dec to Mar), when temperatures can be extremely low. Whistler and Sunshine Village near Banff usually accumulate good amounts of snow.

The weather on the west coast is tempered by the Pacific Ocean. Summers are not too hot, winters are mild, but both seasons can be extremely wet.

WHAT YOU NEED

● Required
○ Suggested
▲ Not required

Some countries require a passport to remain valid for a minimum period (usually at least six months) beyond the date of entry – contact their consulate or embassy or your travel agent for details.

	UK	Germany	USA	Netherlands	Spain
Passport (or National Identity Card where applicable)	●	●	●	●	●
Visa (regulations can change – check before you travel)	▲	▲	▲	▲	▲
Onward or Return Ticket	●	●	▲	●	●
Health Inoculations (tetanus and polio)	▲	▲	▲	▲	▲
Health Documentation (➤ 23, Health Insurance)	▲	▲	▲	▲	▲
Travel Insurance	●	●	▲	●	●
Driving Licence (national)	●	●	●	●	●
Car Insurance Certificate	●	●	●	●	●
Car Registration Document	●	●	●	●	●

WEBSITES

Travel Alberta:
www.travelalberta.com
Tourism British Columbia:
www.hellobc.com
Travel Manitoba:
www.travelmanitoba.com
Northwest Territories Tourism:
www.explorenwt.com
Nunavut Tourism:
www.nunavuttourism.com
Tourism Saskatchewan:
www.sasktourism.com

TOURIST OFFICES AT HOME

In the UK PO Box 101, Chard, Somerset, TA20 9AR
☎ 0870 380 0070
www.canada.travel

In the USA There is no phone or postal contact/office for the general public (www.canada.travel)

In Australia Canadian Tourism Commission ✉ Suite 105, Jones Bay Wharf, 26–32 Pirrama Road, Pyrmont, NSW 2009
☎ (02) 9571-1644

HEALTH INSURANCE

Canada's health system is not free for visitors, and can be expensive. It is advisable to arrange full health coverage, including a "repatriation" clause in case no suitable treatment is available. Keep all bills and receipts to make a claim.

Dental care is also excellent but costly, so include this in your insurance. Most hotels can recommend a dentist, or try the tourist office or Yellow Pages. Again, keep all documentation for your claim.

TIME DIFFERENCES

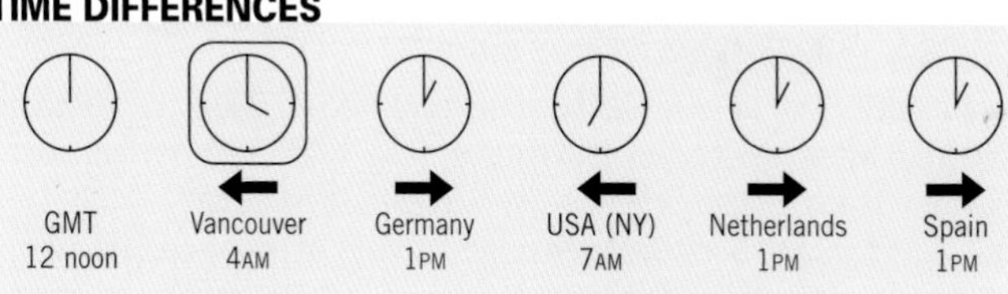

There are four time zones in the region – Eastern (GMT-5), Central (-6), Mountain (-7) and Pacific (-8). Since 2007, clocks go forward one hour on the second Sunday in March for daylight saving time, and back on the first Sunday in November. Saskatchewan uses Central Standard Time all year.

NATIONAL HOLIDAYS

January 1 *New Year's Day*
March/April *Good Friday*
May (Mon preceding May 25) *Victoria Day*
July 1 *Canada Day*
September (1st Mon) *Labor Day*
October (2nd Mon) *Thanksgiving*
December 25 *Christmas Day*

Provincial/territorial holidays
July 9 *Nunavut Day* (Nunavut)
August (1st Mon) *Heritage Day* (AB); *British Columbia Day* (BC); *Civic Holiday* (MB, SK, NWR, Nunavut)
August (3rd Mon) *Discovery Day* (YK)

Other holidays
March/April *Easter Monday*
November 11 *Remembrance Day*
December 26 *Boxing Day*

WHAT'S ON WHEN

January/February *Chinese New Year:* The third-largest Chinese community in North America celebrates in style here, with lion dances at numerous city locations and other events centered on the Dr. Sun Yat-Sen Classical Chinese Garden. Vancouver, British Columbia (www.vancouverchinatown.ca)
February *Yukon Quest International Sled Dog Race:* A 1,646km (1,023-mile) race between Whitehorse and Fairbanks (Alaska). Whitehorse, Yukon (www.yukonquest.com)
March *Vancouver International Dance Festival:* Nearly three weeks of shows featuring local, national and international dancers, with films and workshops.Vancouver, British Columbia (www.vidf.ca)
Royal Manitoba Winter Fair: Six-day agricultural show. Brandon, Manitoba (www.brandonfairs.com)
March/April *Brant Wildlife Festival:* See more than 20,000 Brant geese en route from Mexico to Alaska, with birdwatching, wildlife art and lectures. Qualicum Beach, British Columbia (www.brantfestival.bc.ca)
April *World Ski and Snowboard Festival:* Ten days of action-packed events featuring Olympic and extreme sports legends, plus live music and other entertainment. Whistler, British Columbia (www.wssf.com)
May *Vancouver International Marathon:* Not only the marathon but also many ancillary events as the whole city seems to be on the move. Vancouver, British Columbia (www.bmovanmarathon.ca)

Vancouver International Children's Festival: Fun entertainment especially for children, with lots of hands-on activities. Vancouver, British Columbia (www.childrensfestival.ca)

June/July *International Jazz Festival:* Ten days of jazz, featuring world-class performers. Vancouver, British Columbia (www.coastaljazz.ca)

ICA FolkFest: Multicultural festival of world music, dance and theater. Victoria, British Columbia (www.icafolkfest.com)

July *Calgary Stampede:* North America's biggest, richest and most dangerous rodeo takes place over 10 days, with big-name concerts and cultural events. Calgary, Alberta (www.calgary-stampede.com)

August *Folkorama:* Canada's largest and longest-running multicultural festival. Winnipeg, Manitoba (www.folklorama.ca)

Vancouver Pride Festival and Parade: the city's gay community stages one of North America's biggest and liveliest celebrations of alternative culture (www.vancouverpride.ca)

September *Vancouver Fringe Festival:* Great theater – hilarious, mysterious and unusual shows. Vancouver, British Columbia (www.vancouverfringe.com)

October *Vancouver International Writers & Readers Festival:* Six days of wonderful words on Vancouver's Granville Island at one of North America's premier literary events (www.writersfest.bc.ca)

November *Canadian Finals Rodeo and Farmfair International:* The city fills with cowboys as Canada's toughest rodeo stars battle for the title; also a huge agricultural show. Edmonton, Alberta (www.canadianfinalsrodeo.ca)

November/December *Whistler Film Festival:* World premiers, celebrity guests and plenty of screening and events make this midwinter film fest increasingly popular (www.whistlerfilmfestival.com)

Getting there

BY AIR

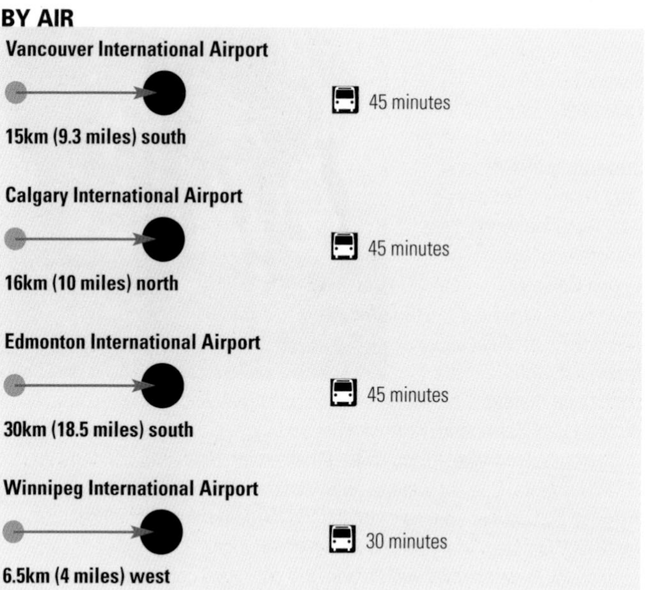

The major airports of Western Canada are Vancouver, Calgary, Edmonton and Winnipeg. Most visitors will arrive at one of them. There are also smaller airports in Regina, Saskatoon, Yellowknife, Whitehorse and Iqaluit. The national airline is Air Canada (tel: 888/247-2262; www.aircanada.ca).

Vancouver International Airport (www.yva.ca) Car or cab – 30 minutes (depending on traffic). Airporter bus (tel: 604/946-8866) every 20 or 30–45 minutes. TransLink bus 424 runs between the airport and the Airport Bus Station (Downtown connections) every seven minutes (www.translink.bc.ca). An urban train line, Canada Line, is scheduled for completion in late 2009 as part of Vancouver's 2010 Winter Olympics infrastructure. It includes a direct link between the airport and Downtown Vancouver (www.canadaline.ca).

Calgary International Airport (www.calgaryairport.com) Car or cab – 30 minutes, Airporter bus (tel: 403/291-9617.

Edmonton International Airport (www.flyeia.com) Car or cab – 35–40 minutes, Sky Shuttle (tel: 780/465-8515).

Winnipeg International Airport (www.waa.ca) Car or cab – 20 minutes (longer in heavy traffic), regular city bus No. 15 (☎ 204/986-5700).

DRIVING

- Drive on the right.
- Speed limits on expressways or highways: 100kph (60mph); on other major roads: 70–90kph (40–55mph); in urban areas and on rural routes: 50kph (30mph) or less.
- Seat belts must be worn by all persons in a vehicle (drivers and passengers) in both the front and back seats.
- Random breath-testing takes place. Never drive under the influence of alcohol.
- Unleaded gas is sold by the liter (leaded gas has been phased out). Gas stations are plentiful on major routes and approaches to cities and stay open until 9 or 10pm (some stay open all night). Away from urban areas, and especially in the North, they may be far apart.
- If you plan on driving in remote areas, it is wise to join the Canadian Automobile Association. British Columbia: tel: 604/268-5555; www.bcaa.com. Alberta: tel: 800/222-6400; www.ama.ab.ca. Saskatchewan: tel: 800/564-6222; www.caasask.sk.ca. Manitoba: tel: 204/262-6100; www.caamanitoba.com.
- The CAA can help in case of breakdown. Card-carrying members of the AAA in the U.S. are entitled to full service with the CAA. Most rental companies provide a rescue service. In case of an emergency, call 911 or 0 depending on your location (➤ 31).

Getting around

PUBLIC TRANSPORTATION

Internal flights Air Canada (tel: 888/247-2262 toll free; www.aircanada.ca), and subsidiaries Jazz (www.flyjazz.ca) and Tango, are the major carriers, servicing every province and territory, with a monopoly on many routes (tel: 888/247-2262 toll free; www.aircanada.ca). WestJet provides a budget air service across Canada and to some U.S. destinations (tel: 403/250-5839, 888/937-8538 toll free; www.westjet.com). Air North (tel: 867/668-2228; www.flyairnorth.com) serves the Yukon from Vancouver, Calgary, Edmonton and Yukon main centers. Harbour Air Seaplanes (tel: 800/665-0212 toll free; www.harbourair.ca) operates between Vancouver and Victoria.

Trains Much of the rail passenger service is provided by VIA Rail (tel: 888/842-7245 toll-free; www.viarail.ca). Trains are clean, fast and efficient, and are a pleasant and scenic way to see the country. In addition, scenic tours are provided on the Rocky Mountaineer and Whistler Mountaineer (tel: 604/606-3200; www.rockymountaineer.com), and the Skeena train between Jasper and Prince Rupert (contact VIA Rail).

Long-distance buses Relatively inexpensive buses give access to most of the region. The major company is Greyhound Canada (tel: 800/661-8747; www.greyhound.ca), with cross-border links to U.S. cities. A Canada Discovery Pass is available for differing lengths of time (tel: 0845/680-1298). There are savings on tickets purchased in advance.

Ferries BC Ferries are the main operators on the Pacific coast (tel: 888/223-3779; www.bcferries.com), including the Inside Passage service (► 128). Three services link the U.S. west coast and BC: Black Ball Ferry Line (tel: 250/386-2202); Clipper Navigation (tel: 250/382-8100); and San Juan Cruises (tel: 360/738-8099, 800/443-4552 toll free; www.whales.com).

Urban transportation In general, all cities in Western Canada have good public transportation systems that make travel relatively easy for visitors. The Vancouver Translink system (tel: 604/953-3333; www.translink.bc.ca) includes buses, trolleys, the SeaBus catamaran ferries and the above-ground SkyTrain rail service.

TAXIS

Taxis are the most costly way to travel, especially in rush-hour traffic. Cabs can be found in stands beside major hotels, at airports, and train and bus stations. They can also be hailed on the street or called by telephone.

CAR RENTAL

All major car rental firms are represented here. To rent, you must be over 21, with ID and a valid driver's license, held for at least a year. You will need a credit card, and to return the vehicle to another site, a sizeable drop-off fee may apply. Most rental cars have automatic transmission.

FARES AND TICKETS

Tickets for flights, train and buses can be purchased online, as well as at airports, stations and ticket agents. The main long-distance bus operator, Greyhound and train operator VIA (➤ opposite) offer unlimited travel passes for various time periods. In Vancouver TransLink (➤ above) tickets are valid for buses, SkyTrain and SeaBus. Tickets are bought directly from bus drivers, but you must have the exact fare. Tickets can be bought from machines for SkyTrain at stations and for SeaBus at ferry terminals or at 7-Eleven stores and other stores displaying a TransLink sticker. Victoria and Calgary have similar ticketing systems for their public transportation services. Most services offer reduced rates for seniors. Age qualifications may differ and you may have to provide proof of age.

Being there

TOURIST OFFICES

- Travel Alberta ✉ PO Box 2500, Edmonton, AB, T5J 2Z4 ☎ 800/252-3782 (toll free); www.travelalberta.com
- Tourism British Columbia ✉ Parliament Buildings, Victoria, BC, V8V 1X4 ☎ 800/HELLOBC (toll free); www.hellobc.com
- Travel Manitoba ✉ 7th Floor, 155 Carlton Street, Winnipeg, MN, R3C 3H8 ☎ 800/665-0040 (toll free); www.travelmanitoba.com
- Northwest Territories Tourism ✉ PO Box 610, Yellowknife, NT, X1A 2N5 ☎ 800/661-0788 (toll free); www.explorenwt.com
- Nunavut Tourism ✉ PO Box 1450, Iqaluit, NU, X0A 0H0 ☎ 866/686-2888; www.nunavuttourism.com
- Tourism Saskatchewan ✉ 1922 Park Street, Regina, SK, S4N 7M4 ☎ 306/787-9600, 877/237-2273 (toll free); www.sasktourism.com
- Tourism Yukon ✉ PO Box 2703, Whitehorse, YK, Y1A 2C6 ☎ 800/661-0494 (toll free); www.touryukon.com

MONEY

Canada's currency is the Canadian dollar (100 cents = $1). Bills come in $5, $10, $20, $50 and $100, but the $100 is often difficult to use – people are suspicious of it due to forgeries. Coins come as pennies (1 cent), nickels (5 cents), dimes (10 cents), quarters (25 cents), loonies ($1 – named for the bird on them) and twoonies or toonies ($2). The $1 coin is gold colored, the $2 coin has a gold center and silver rim.

Exchange rates are variable so check the current rate just before leaving on a trip. Although credit and debit cards are widely accepted, it is best to check whether your card is accepted before making purchases.

TIPS/GRATUITIES

Yes ✓ No ✕		
Restaurants (if service not included)	✓	15–20%
Cafés/bars (if service not included)	✓	10%
Taxis	✓	10%
Tour guides	✓	$2
Washrooms/restrooms	✕	
Hotel service staff	✓	10%

POSTAL AND INTERNET SERVICES

Mail boxes are generally red with the words Canada Post/Postes Canada written on them.

Internet facilities are well established in Canadian cities, where you will find Internet cafés. Many hotels either have WiFi or manual connections in their rooms, or a terminal in the foyer.

TELEPHONES

Outdoor public telephones are located in glass and metal booths. To make a call, lift the handset, insert the correct coin (25¢ or $1 coins), a telephone credit card or a prepaid calling card (available in post offices, convenience stores, newsagents etc), and then dial.

Emergency telephone numbers

For police, fire department and ambulance services:
In Manitoba, Saskatchewan, Alberta and mainland British Columbia: ☎ 911.

In Vancouver Island, Yukon, Northwest Territories and Nunavut: ☎ 0 for operator and say that it is an emergency.

International dialing codes

From Western Canada to:
USA: 1
UK: 011 44
Australia: 011 61
France: 011 33

EMBASSIES

In the Canadian Federal capital of Ottawa:
USA 490 Sussex Drive ☎ 613/238-5335; www.usembassycanada.gov
UK 80 Elgin Street ☎ 613/237-1530; www.britainincanada.org
Australia 50 O'Connor Street, Suite 710 ☎ 613/236-0841; www.ahc-ottawa.org
France 42 Sussex Drive ☎ 613/789-1795; www.ambafrance-ca.org

ELECTRICITY

Voltage in Canada is 110v. Sockets require plugs with two (or three) flat prongs. Visitors from outside North America need an adaptor. Razors, hairdriers and laptops are usually dual-voltage, but correct plugs are needed.

HEALTH AND SAFETY

Sun advice The Prairies have hot summers so use sunscreen and wear sunglasses. These are needed in the North too. In winter the reflection off the snow can cause serious sunburn.

Drugs Carry a supply of any prescription you have to take. Over-the-counter drugs are readily available, but no Canadian pharmacy will accept an out-of-province prescription. You would have to visit a Canadian doctor and get a new prescription that's recognized locally.

Safe water It is safe to drink tap water in Canada. Bottled water is widely available. When camping, boil drinking water for 10 minutes as protection against "beaver fever", caused by a parasite found in lakes and streams.

Personal safety Although Western Canada is remarkably crime-free, a few simple precautions will help prevent unfortunate incidents.

- Don't leave bags or other valuables visible in your car.
- Don't wear expensive jewelry or carry large sums of money.
- Carry credit cards and passports in a pouch or belt.
- Walk only along well-lit streets at night.

The Royal Canadian Mounted Police (RCMP) are the federal police force and they ensure regular police work in all four Western provinces and in the three territories. All major cities also have their own police forces.

OPENING HOURS

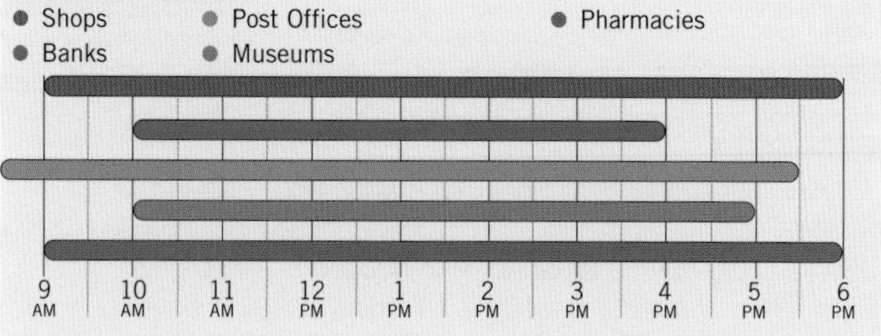

Some stores do not open on Sunday. Supermarkets and malls open longer. Some branches of banks open earlier and some stay open to 5 or 6pm on Thursday or Friday. Some convenience stores sell stamps and may be open later than 5:30pm and on Saturday morning. Most museums are closed Monday. Major museums stay open until 9pm one evening a week. Major cities have pharmacies open 24-hours a day.

LANGUAGE

Canada is officially a bilingual English/French country. There are French-speaking communities in all four Western provinces, but they are quite small compared with the number of French speakers in Eastern Canada. You will not need to learn any French while traveling in Western Canada.

Inuktitut is the language of the Inuit peoples of the Northwest Territories and Nunavut. In the NWT (western and central Arctic), Roman orthography is used. In Nunavut (eastern Arctic), Inuktitut is written using symbols called syllabics to represent different sounds. Here are a few useful Inuktitut expressions using Roman orthography.

ENGLISH	INUKTITUT	PRONUNCIATION
How are you?	*Qanuipit?*	(Ka-nwee-peet?)
I'm fine	*Qanuingittunga*	(Ka-nweeng-ni-toon-ga)
What's your name?	*Kinauvit?*	(Kee-nau-veet?)
Thank you	*Qujannamiik*	(Coo-yan-na-mee-ick)
You're welcome	*Ilaali*	(Ee-lah-lih)
Yes/No	*Ii/Aakka* or *aagaa*	(Ee)/(Ah-ka or Ah-ga)
Maybe (I don't really know)	*Atsuuli* or *aamai*	(At-soo-lee or Ah-my)
Goodbye (to one person)	*Tavvauvutit*	(Tah-vow-voo-teet)
Goodbye (to a group)	*Tavvauvusi*	(Tah-vow-voo-see)
How much is it?	*Qatsituqqa?*	(Cat-see-to-kaw?)
How many?	*Qatsiit?*	(Cat-seet?)
I'm cold	*Qiuliqtunga*	(K-o-lick-toon-ga)
It's cold (weather)	*Ikkiirnaqtuq*	(Ick-eang-nak-took)
Will the weather be good today?	*Silasianguniapa?*	(See-la-see-aang-un-ee-aa-pa?)
I'm hungry	*Kaaktunga*	(Kak-toon-ga)
Help!	*Ikajunga!*	(Ick-a-yung-ga!)
I'm sick	*Aaniajunga*	(Ah-nee-a-yung-ga)
Where am I?	*Namiippunga?*	(Nah-me-poon-ga?)
Where's the hotel?	*Nau taima sinitavik?*	(Naowk tie-ma see-nee-ta-vik?)
I'd like to use the washroom	*Quisuktunga*	(Kwee-soot-toon-ga)

Best places to see

1 Banff National Park

www.pc.gc.ca/banff

Canada's oldest national park is arguably its most beautiful, with sublime scenery, emerald lakes and majestic snow-covered mountains.

Banff National Park was created in the mid-1880s to protect and preserve the hot springs discovered gushing from Sulphur Mountain during construction of the Canadian Pacific Railway. Within its boundaries are the mountain resorts of Banff and Lake Louise, two scenic highways, forests and countless magnificent viewpoints and waterfalls.

Most visitors use Banff Townsite (➤ 90) as a base for exploring the park. From here it's 60km

(37 miles) northwest to **Lake Louise** (➤ 98), following the TransCanada (Highway 1) or the Bow Valley Parkway (Highway 1A), a more relaxed and scenic alternative, with lots of pulloffs, viewpoints and trails. Look for elk, moose and bears.

A highlight on Bow Valley Parkway is Johnston Canyon, 32km (20 miles) west of Banff, which can be seen on the Johnston Canyon Trail (2.7km/ 1.7 miles each way). Here you can walk to two pretty waterfalls.

From Lake Louise, Highway 1 heads west into Yoho National Park (➤ 105), while the scenic Icefields Parkway (➤ 102–103), one of the world's greatest drives, runs north to Jasper (➤ 94) in Jasper National Park (➤ 44–45).

The park's lakes are justly famous, and 13km (8 miles) east of Lake Louise is Moraine Lake (➤ 98), a beautiful spot at the foot of the Wenkchemna Mountains.

There are plenty of opportunities year-round to pursue outdoor activities – guided hikes, river-rafting, kayaking and golf in summer; downhill and Nordic skiing, tobogganing, snowmobiling and sleigh rides in winter.

✚ 17K
ℹ Information Centre ✉ 224 Banff Avenue, Banff, Alberta ☎ 403/762-1550 ⏲ Late Jun–early Sep daily 8–8; mid-May to late Jun, early Sep to mid-Sep daily 9–7; mid-Sep to mid-May daily 9–5

Lake Louise Visitor Centre
✉ Lake Louise village, Alberta ☎ 403/522-3833 ⏲ Late Jun to mid-Sep daily 9–7/8; mid-Sep to late Jun daily 9–4/5

2 Butchart Gardens

www.butchartgardens.com

These stunning gardens, planted with rare and exotic species, are possibly the most spectacular floral display on the continent.

In 1904, Jenny Butchart, the wife of Robert Pim Butchart, a pioneer in the manufacture of Portland cement in Canada, began to develop and landscape the abandoned area created by a worked out quarry from his business. The result is one of the loveliest gardens imaginable and an unmissable stop. The 22ha (55-acre) gardens lie 22km (13.5 miles) north of Central Victoria, in Brentwood Bay, and contain more than a million individual plants, trees and shrubs representing some 700 different species, collected from around the world.

Jenny's earliest work, the Sunken Gardens, is set 25m (82ft) below ground level on the floor of the original quarry and is filled with a magnificent collection of flowers, shrubs and classical statuary. The Rose Garden, planted with hybrid tea roses around a wishing well, is best visited in July and August when the air is heavy with the scent of the blooms. Next comes the Japanese Garden, with its rare Himalayan blue poppies, laid out in 1906 with the help of a Japanese landscape gardener. Last is the Italian Garden, the most formal of them all, on the site of the Butcharts' tennis court.

There's something to see at any time of year – including fall foliage and winter berries. It can get very busy at times and you are almost forced along, as if on a conveyor belt. Late afternoons

are generally the best time of day to visit, when most of the tour buses have left. The excellent gift store sells a range of seeds, plants and garden accessories, along with excellent First Nations crafts and souvenirs.

14L 800 Benvenuto Avenue, Brentwood Bay, Vancouver Island, British Columbia 866/652-4422, 250/652-5256 (recorded information) Daily from 9am (from 1pm Dec 25). Closing time varies seasonally from 3:30pm Jan/Feb to 10pm mid-Jun to early Sep Expensive Coffee shop ($), Blue Poppy Restaurant ($–$$), Dining Room ($$$)

3 Howe Sound

www.squamishchamber.bc.com

The drive from Vancouver along the Sea to Sky Highway reveals awe-inspiring views of unspoiled scenery.

The beautiful, fjord-like coastline of Howe Sound was formed by water erosion, volcanic activity and receding glaciers. To reach it from Vancouver, head across the North Shore of Burrard Inlet and go west on Route 1. This links with the Sea to Sky Highway (Route 99), a spectacular drive along the twisting shores of the Sound, past bays and coves, snow-capped peaks and alpine lakes encircled by firs, on its way to Whistler (➤ 104–105). As an alternative to driving you can take a leisurely cruise.

It's no longer possible to take the railroad along the coast, but you can visit the **West Coast Railway Heritage Park** in Squamish, at the head of Howe Sound, a must-see for train enthusiasts. Squamish is not a particularly attractive town, but it offers a wide range of outdoor activities including mountaineering, watersports, horseback riding and spelunking (caving).

The **British Columbia Museum of Mining** at Britannia Beach is a popular attraction. The copper mine was established in 1899 and in its heyday in the 1920s and 1930s it was the most productive in the British Empire. It closed in 1974 and reopened the following year as this museum, with mine tours, an interpretive center and a fascinating account of the mine's history.

15L
Squamish Visitor Information Service
PO Box 1009, 38551 Loggers Lane, Squamish, British Columbia 604/815-4994 Daily 9–5

West Coast Railway Heritage Park
Squamish, British Columbia 604/898-9336; www.wcra.org Daily 10–5
Moderate

British Columbia Museum of Mining
PO Box 188, Britannia Beach, British Columbia 604/896-2233; www.bcmuseumofmining.org Early May to mid-Oct daily 9–4:30; mid-Oct to early May Mon–Fri 9–4:30 Summer: expensive; winter: moderate

4 Icefields Parkway

This 230km (143-mile) route between Lake Louise and Jasper is one of the world's most spectacular mountain highways.

Officially Route 93, the Icefields Parkway runs through the heart of Banff and Jasper national parks (➤ 36–37 and 44–45), offering endless vistas of snow-capped mountains, interspersed with shimmering lakes, waterfalls and rivers, and the icefields (glaciers) after which it is named.

The whole length of the parkway is a never-ending series of sublime views, but there are some highlights to look for. Along the first stretch from Lake Louise to Bow Summit are Hector Lake, the second largest lake in Banff National Park, and Crowfoot Glacier, the first of a series of superb glaciers. Bow Lake has one of the best lake walks, the Bow Lake and Bow Glacier Falls Trail, and there are stunning panoramas from Peyto Lake Lookout. Mistaya Canyon is an excellent example of a landscape eroded by the action of water.

Saskatchewan River Crossing, just north of Bow Summit, is the last place to fill up with gas before Jasper. You'll also find refreshments and accommodations here, or

you can take the David Thompson Highway east to the small town of Rocky Mountain House, a good place for an overnight stop.

Continuing north, you come to the Columbia Icefields, the largest sub-polar sheet of ice and snow in North America, covering around 324sq km (125sq miles) and about 305m (1,000ft) deep. It sits on the continental divide and its meltwater flows into the Arctic, Pacific and Atlantic oceans. From the Columbia Icefields Centre "Snocoaches" take you to the middle of the Athabasca Glacier, where you can step out onto the ice. Don't be tempted to go out on your own; hidden cliffs and holes covered by a thin layer of snow are deadly hazards.

Two more highlights stand out before reaching Jasper: the Sunwapta Falls, and the Athabasca Falls (the most photogenic of the two), respectively 56 and 29km (35 and 18 miles) from Jasper.

17K

Columbia Icefields Centre Icefields Parkway, Jasper, Alberta 403/762-6700, 877/423-7433 (toll free); www.columbiaicefield.com May to mid-Oct daily 9–5/6

5 Jasper National Park

www.pc.gc.ca/jasper
www.jaspercanadianrockies.com

The natural beauty, wildlife and outdoor activities of Canada's largest national park should tempt you to linger and explore.

Jasper National Park covers an area of 10,880sq km (4,200sq miles), greater than the three other Canadian Rockies' parks combined. Jasper Townsite (➤ 94) is the perfect base for visiting the park, and its visitor center opposite the train station gives an excellent introduction.

The 48km (30-mile) Maligne Lake Road is a good place to spot elk, deer, bighorn sheep, coyote and black bears, especially early or late in the day. It passes Maligne Canyon, up to 55m (180ft) deep and the most spectacular of the accessible canyons in the Rockies. An easy trail loops down part of the canyon from the parking area, taking you past several waterfalls. Medicine Lake, 14km (8.5 miles) farther, is unusual for the fluctuations in its water level; sometimes the lake "disappears" due to an underground drainage system. At the end of the road is Maligne Lake, the largest and most beautiful lake in the Rockies (➤ 50–51).

Miette Hot Springs, northeast of Jasper Townsite, are the hottest springs in the Canadian Rockies, emerging at a temperature of 54°C (129°F), but they are cooled to a more comfortable 40°C (104°F) as they enter the pool complex.

Running through the heart of the park, from Lake Louise in adjoining Banff National Park, is the Icefields Parkway (➤ 42–43).

17K

Jasper National Park Information Centre 500 Connaught Drive, Jasper, Alberta 780/852-6176 Mid-Jun to Labour Day daily 8:30–7; Labour Day–Sep daily 9–6; Apr to mid-Jun, Oct daily 9–5; rest of year daily 9–4

Park permits: moderate

6 Manitoba Museum

www.manitobamuseum.ca

Winnipeg's spectacular heritage center explores humankind's complex relationship with the natural environment.

The Centennial Centre (➤ 136) is home to the Manitoba Museum, which opened in 1974 to commemorate the city's centennial. A series of interpretive galleries allows you to experience the sights and sounds of Manitoba, from its earliest known history to the present day.

Begin in the Orientation Gallery, where a wonderful life-size diorama of stampeding bison sets the scene for the theme of the museum. The Earth History Gallery examines Manitoba's geology, from the tropical fossils found in the earth to marine skeletons from 800 million years ago. In the Sub-Arctic Gallery a diorama highlights the life of the northern Inuit, who live by hunting caribou. Look for the polar bears. The Boreal Forest Gallery recreates the landscape that covers almost a third of the province, and shows moose grazing the tall grasses among the coniferous vegetation.

An outstanding feature is the Nonsuch Gallery. It celebrates the coming of Europeans with a life-size recreation of the two-masted ketch *Nonsuch*, which sailed into Hudson's Bay in 1668 to found the fur trade in Canada. This replica was built in England in 1970 to commemorate the 300th anniversary of the Hudson's Bay Company. You can board the ship in the replicated 17th-century Thames River port, then experience the lifestyle

of the fur traders in the Hudson's Bay Company Gallery next door.

The Grasslands Gallery looks at the effect European settlers had on the prairies. Brace yourself for the Garter Snake Pit. The Urban Gallery traces the rise of Winnipeg and its role in the westward expansion of the pioneers. Pride of place here goes to the bustling 1920s-style street, complete with stores, railroad, theater and movie house. In the separate Power Level you'll find more than 100 hands-on exhibits in the popular Science Gallery, including Water World, and in the Planetarium you can explore the night sky and take a virtual journey to the stars.

24M 190 Rupert Avenue, Winnipeg, Manitoba 204/956-2830 Mid-May to early Sep daily 10–5; early Sep to mid-May Tue–Fri 10–4, Sat–Sun 11–5 Moderate. Combined ticket for museum, planetarium and science gallery: expensive

Museum of Anthropology

www.moa.ubc.ca

Vancouver's finest museum has seen extensive renovation and expansion that is due for partial completion by fall 2009 and for complete relaunch in January 2010. It is a superb showcase dedicated to the culture of the local Haida, Salish, Tsimshian and Kwaiutt First Nations.

This museum was the first to treat the lifestyle and art of the First Nations people with the same respect as that of European history, a move that has since been adopted throughout Canada. Arthur Erickson designed the building in 1976, and his inspiration was the traditional post-and-beam

wooden dwellings of the Kwakwaka'wakw people. It is one of the finest examples of modern architecture, whose breathtaking glass-walled, top-lit Great Hall makes a perfect setting for the unrivaled collection of totem poles. Through the large glass windows you can look out on to more totems in the gardens, beautifully framed by the waters of the Georgia Strait.

Alongside the Great Hall are other galleries where you will find a fine collection of intricately carved works in silver, gold, argillite, bone and wood, along with ceremonial masks.

Perhaps the museum's single greatest exhibit is the acclaimed cedar sculpture *The Raven and the First Men* in the Rotunda, by world-renowned Haida artist Bill Reid (1920–98). Weighing more than 4 tons, it is dominated by a raven sitting on top of a clamshell, while human figures try to escape from it.

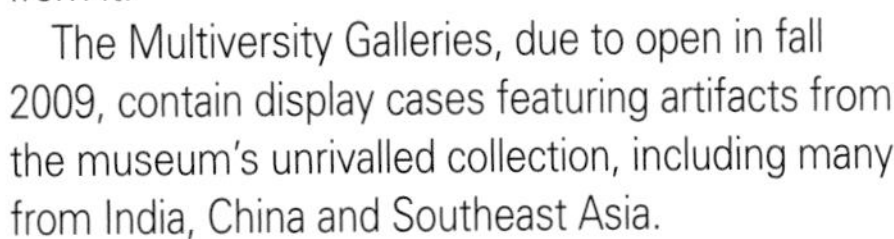

The Multiversity Galleries, due to open in fall 2009, contain display cases featuring artifacts from the museum's unrivalled collection, including many from India, China and Southeast Asia.

While you are here, turn right out of the museum for a short walk to the small Nitobe Memorial Garden (open daily; inexpensive), considered the most authentic Japanese garden outside Japan.

Vancouver 1f (off map) 6393 Northwest Marine Drive, University of British Columbia Campus, Vancouver, British Columbia 604/822-5087 Mid-May to early Sep daily 10–5 (also Tue 5–9); early Sep to mid-May Tue–Sun 11–5 (also Tue 5–9) Moderate Café ($) 4, 9, 17, 25, 41, 43, 44, 49, 99, 258, 480

8 Rocky Mountain Lakes

The lakes that nestle among the peaks of the Rockies are renowned for their fabulous colors and sublime settings.

Many of the lakes owe their intense color to the presence of superfine particles of glacial silt, known as rock flour. When this is suspended in the water it absorbs all incoming light except for the turquoise-blue spectrum. The varying amount in each lake accounts for the wide difference in color, which also changes during the year. In spring there is little rock flour in the water so they are much the same color as other lakes, but as glacial material flows into them during the summer melt, they take on their individual hues once again.

Lake Louise (➤ 98) in Banff National Park is a peerless, sapphire lake, backed by mountains, glaciers and tumbling forests. For fantastic views take the Lake Louise Gondola that runs

up Mount Whitehorn, just east of Lake Louise Village.

Just 13km (8 miles) south of Lake Louise is Moraine Lake (➤ 98). Much smaller, its water is a deeper blue, and the stupendous snow-dusted Wenkchemna Mountains create a more spectacular backdrop. Stroll along the lakeshore or take the short walk to Consolation Lake.

Maligne Lake in Jasper National Park (➤ 44–45), the largest lake in the Rockies and the second deepest after Upper Waterton Lake (➤ 100), is a wonderful ensemble of water, forest and mountain. Most visitors drive or take a tour along the road, then join one of the 90-minute boat trips on the lake.

Beautiful Emerald Lake is one of the quieter spots in the Rockies. It's easily accessed from Field, which lies at the heart of Yoho National Park (➤ 105).

Peyto Lake Lookout in Banff National Park is a highlight of the Icefields Parkway (➤ 42–43), and has one of the most impressive panoramas in the Rockies, overlooking Peyto Lake, which nestles at the base of the surrounding mountains.

17K ✉ Information for the lakes may be found on pages cross-referenced within text; otherwise visit www.pc.gc.ca for full details of Canada's national and provincial parks

9 Royal Tyrrell Museum

www.tyrrellmuseum.com

A highlight of the Alberta Badlands and devoted entirely to dinosaurs, this museum offers an incredible experience for all ages.

The Tyrrell is one of the finest museums of its kind, located about 6km (4.5 miles) northwest of Drumheller, so-called "dinosaur capital of the world" (► 156–157). It takes its name from Joseph Tyrrell, who accidentally stumbled across the bones of an *Albertosaurus* amid the scrub and sagebrush of the Badlands in 1884. This was the first of several hundred complete dinosaur skeletons that have since been excavated, and more are unearthed just about every year.

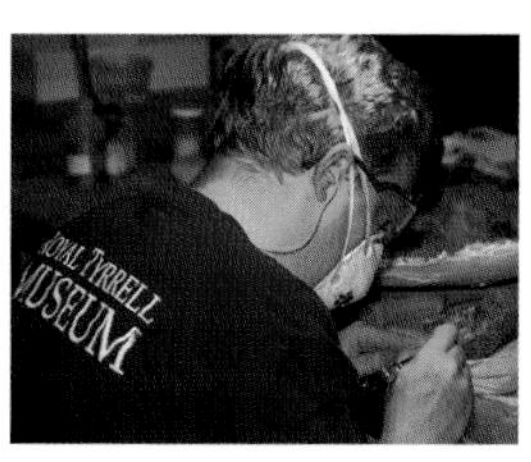

The museum exhibits around 35 of them, all strikingly presented in replicated natural surroundings, including the original *Albertosaurus*. *Tyrannosaurus rex* is a predictable favorite, along with more unusual dinosaurs, such as *Xiphactinus*, and *Quetzalcoatlus*, believed to be the largest flying creature ever to have existed. The paleontology collection covers 3.9 billion years and includes some dramatic specimens from the Mesozoic era.

Computers and videos bring prehistory to life, and other attractions include state-of-the-art displays on the evolution of life on earth, and a primeval garden that reproduces the indigenous

vegetation of 350 million years ago. You can also watch scientists at work on fossils in the on-site laboratories, and learn more about Yoho National Park's Burgess Shales fossil beds (➤ 105).

A visit to the museum is best taken in conjunction with a trip to the Dinosaur Provincial Park (➤ 156), where you will find one of the museum's field stations.

18L Highway 838, Midland Provincial Park, 6km (4 miles) northwest of Drumheller, Alberta 403/823-7707, 403/823-7707 (toll free in Alberta); 888/440-4240 (toll free in North America – outisde Alberta) Mid-May to early Sep daily 9–9; early Sep to mid-Oct daily 10–5; mid-Oct to mid-May Tue–Sun 10–5 Moderate Cafeteria ($)

10 Stanley Park

www.vancouver.ca

You can't come to Vancouver and not visit Stanley Park, one of the world's greatest urban open spaces, and an oasis close to the heart of the city's busy downtown.

Stanley Park was set aside as permanent public parkland in 1888 when the British Government handed its 405ha (1,000 acres) over to the city. This semi-wilderness of dense rain forest, woodland

glades and marshland juts out into Burrard Inlet, with water on three sides. On the park's eastern fringe are the more manicured gardens and a medley of sights and self-contained attractions, including the Lost Lagoon, a shallow tidal haven for birds such as scaup, cormorants, mergansers; the 5,000-bush Rose Garden; and the Vancouver Aquarium (➤ 84–85).

A horse-drawn bus is great for getting an overview of Stanley Park, and in summer there's a free shuttle bus, but the best way to really appreciate what the park offers is to walk, cycle or roller-blade the 16km (10-mile) Sea Wall that circles the park. Even if you don't do the whole circuit you should enjoy the superlative views from some part of it. Prospect Point, perched on a cliff at the northern tip of the park, is the highest point, and from here you can see the North Shore (➤ 82–83), and out into the Pacific beyond English Bay. The sandy beaches come as a real surprise, being so close to the downtown area of this huge metropolis.

The park has plenty of activities that are suitable for all ages, including the Children's Farmyard, a miniature railroad, a water park, a heated oceanside swimming pool and the Theatre under the Stars.

Vancouver 1a (off map) Western tip of downtown Vancouver, British Columbia 604/257-8400 Freely accessible Free Cafés along seawall at Prospect Point and Ferguson Point 19, 135, Express Bus (fare refunded in vouchers for admission to various park attractions)

Best things to do

Great places to have lunch

Alycia's

Menu reflects the West's Ukrainian heritage – *pirogis*, cabbage rolls and *kolbassa* sausages.

✉ 559 Cathedral Avenue, Winnipeg ☎ 204/582-8789

Beachcombers

Great al-fresco eating on The Forks riverside where Beachcombers offers Caribbean-flavored salads, seafood and meat dishes on a big patio or in a cosy indoor setting.

✉ The Forks, Winnipeg ☎ 204/948-0020

Brioche

Mixed seafood, quiches and salads are just some of the treats available at this popular eatery.

✉ 401 West Cordova Street, Vancouver ☎ 604/682-4037

Bullock's Bistro

Tiny place, tiny menu – try the pan-fried fish or caribou steaks.

✉ 3534 Weaver Drive, Yellowknife ☎ 867/873-3474

Bushwakker Brewing Co Ltd

Big, breezy brewpub serving gourmet pizzas and steaks, as well as treats such as shrimp remoulade.

✉ 2206 Dewdney Avenue, Regina ☎ 306/359-7276

Buzzards Cowboy Cuisine

Features such traditional Western delicacies as slow roasted barbecued pulled beef on a bun.

✉ 140 10th Avenue SW, Calgary ☎ 403/264-6959

Da-De-O

1950s-style diner that serves up Cajun favorites like New Orleans sandwiches and blackened catfish.

✉ 10548A 82nd Avenue, Edmonton ☎ 780/433-0930

Red Fish Blue Fish

This take-out fish restaurant, with some quayside seating, offers fish and chips with class, including halibut, wild salmon and Fanny Bay oysters.

✉ Broughton Street Pier, Wharf Street, Victoria ☎ 250/298-6877

Tony's Fish & Oyster Café

Granville Island landmark serving fresh oysters, and huge seafood platters that are ideal for sharing.

✉ 1511 Anderson Street, Vancouver ☎ 604/683-7127

Wanuskewin Restaurant

Lunch on bison stew, wild rice salad or jumbo hot dogs in a room overlooking the beautiful Opimihaw Valley.

✉ Wanuskewin Heritage Park, Saskatoon ☎ 306/931-6767

Top activities

- **Birding and wildlife watching** (➤ 11).
- **Climbing** in the Rockies.
- **Golf** The Top of the World Golf Course is Canada's most northerly course.
- **Hiking** Especially in Banff, Jasper and Yoho national parks (➤ 36–37, 44–45 and 105).
- **Horseback riding** Dude ranches and opportunities for trail riding dot the West and Yukon.

- **Sailing** off the British Columbia coast and on Great Slave Lake.
- **Salmon fishing** Permits required.
- **Skiing** Alberta and British Columbia resorts are among the world's best, with Whistler set to host the Winter Olympics in 2010.
- **Whale-watching** trip from the harbor in Victoria (➤ 115).
- **Whitewater rafting** The most challenging runs are in northern British Columbia and Yukon.

THE RENDEZVOUS
CAUTION

Best parks

Banff National Park
Canada's first national park (Alberta, ➤ 36–37) preserves stunning lakes, hot springs, vast forests and mountain peaks.

Cypress Hills Inter-Provincial Park
The only park in Canada that spans provincial boundaries (Saskatchewan and Alberta, ➤ 154–155), this is a breathtaking area of highlands, pine forests and rushing rivers.

Gwaii Haanas National Park Reserve
This remote island wilderness in the Pacific (British Columbia, ➤ 127) preserves priceless ecological treasures and the ancient culture of the artistic Haida people.

Kluane National Park
High, craggy mountains, mighty glaciers and verdant valleys surround Canada's highest mountains (Yukon, ➤ 178).

Pacific Rim National Park
Trapped between the Insular Mountains and the wild Pacific, this park (British Columbia, ➤ 124–125) protects coastal rain forests, dunes and pristine beaches with rich marine life.

Unusual activities

Glacier skiing
To engage in winter sports at the height of summer, head for Whistler (British Columbia, ➤ 104–105) and enjoy the fine powdery snow that's kept cool by the Horstman glacier on Blackcomb Mountain.

Gold panning
Recreate for yourself a little bit of the famous Klondike gold rush. There are places around Dawson City (Yukon, ➤ 172) where you can still pan for gold and keep what you find.

Kayaking among orcas
The most exciting whale-watching you can get is to kayak among the resident orcas that inhabit the protected waters between mainland British Columbia and northern Vancouver Island. Expect to see other kinds of whales, dolphins and eagles, too.

Midnight rides
In summer the sun never sets on the Yukon, and you can enjoy the wonderful scenery on horseback into the night.

Polar bear watching
One of Canada's biggest adventures is to go to Churchill (Manitoba, ➤ 152) when the polar bears are around, between July/early August and November. Special buggies get you up close to the bears.

In high places

The spectacular mountains, forests and wild coastline of Western Canada offer a paradise of opportunity for outdoor leisure at all levels. There are outstanding opportunities for watersports such as canoeing and whitewater rafting and for horse riding and mountain biking. There are also specialist activities from snowboarding to dog-sledding, kite flying to the latest craze, zip lining, a wild ride down an inclined cable. Yet, the simplest activities of all are still walking and hiking.

- If all you want is a casual stroll in great surroundings, you can follow low-level, surfaced walkways of only a kilometer or two (0.5–1.2 miles) at venues such as Johnston Canyon and Edith Cavell Meadows Trail in **Jasper National Park** (➤ 44–45), although you share the experience with scores of fellow visitors.
- For a more remote experience there are superb day hikes in most of the parks. You can escape the overcrowded Lake Louise shoreline by heading uphill to the Lake Agnes Teahouse (➤ 96–97) and can extend the hike to the Plain of Six Glaciers trail that leads high into the awesome mountains encircling Lake Louise. In **Yoho National Park** (➤ 105) the superb 20km (12.5-mile) Iceline Trail takes steep zigzags that lead to the high moraine of several glaciers overlooking the 256m-high (840ft) Takakkaw Falls.
- The ultimate high-places experience is to tackle a multi-day hike to a back-country campsite or lodge or head along the splendid West Coast Trail in the **Pacific Rim National Park** (➤ 124–125) on Vancouver Island. You need to plan ahead for these, book campsites and get permits from the National Park authorities, often some time in advance.

All of the National Park websites have information, advice and guidance about outdoor activities of all types.
www.pc.gc.ca/pn-np/ab/jasper
www.pc.gc.ca/yoho
www.pc.gc.ca/pacificrim

Stunning viewpoints

Emerald Lake (➤ 105)

Hell's Gate Air Tram (➤ 92, 93)

Icefields Parkway (➤ 42–43)

Jasper Tramway (➤ 94)

Lake Agnes (➤ 96–97)

Lake Louise Gondola (➤ 98)

Maligne Lake (➤ 44)

Moraine Lake (➤ 98)

Pacific Rim National Park (➤ 124–125)

Peyto Lake Lookout (➤ 51)

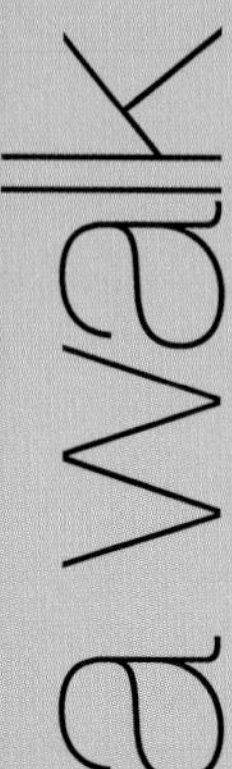

in downtown Vancouver

This walk across downtown includes shopping streets (Burrard and Robson), the cathedral, the Bill Reid Gallery and Vancouver Art Gallery.

Start at Canada Place (➤ 79).

The impressive cruise ship terminus offers majestic views north across the waters of Burrard Inlet and Coal Harbour.

Walk from the waterfront down Burrard Street to the 19th-century, neo-Gothic Christ Church Cathedral.

The cathedral sits on the corner of Burrard and Georgia. Turn left here, past Hotel Vancouver on the opposite corner.

Turn left along Georgia Street to its junction with Hornby Street.

Divert left down Hornby Street to the Bill Reid Gallery of Northwest Coast Art. Back at the junction cross over and visit the HSBC bank's Atrium Gallery reception area, with its massive pendulum and art displays.

Continue southwest down Hornby Street.

The vibrant Vancouver Art Gallery (➤ 86–87) is midway down on the east side of the street.

Where Robson Street intersects Hornby, turn left.

After five blocks the Public Library appears on the left on the corner of Robson and Homer.

Turn right on Homer Street.

Look for the BC Place Stadium, which comes into view on the left down intersecting streets as you stroll.

*Pass the Chintz and Company store on the left, then turn left on Nelson Street into Yaletown. This rundown warehouse district was transformed in the 1990s into the trendiest area of the downtown peninsula. Head to the corner of Hamilton and Davie streets and go right. Walk uphill to rejoin Hornby Street; turn left to the waterfront for the Aquabus to Granville Island (**► 81**).*

Distance 3.2 km (2 miles)
Time 1.5 hours (not including tours and shopping)
Start point Canada Place ✚ *Vancouver 7b*
End point Aquabus terminal, Hornby Street ✚ *Vancouver 3e*
Lunch Yaletown Brewing Company ($$) ✉ 1111 Mainland Street
☎ 604/681-2739

Best shopping

CLOTHES AND ACCESSORIES

Alberta Boot

Thousands of boots and shoes made from cow hide, alligator, kangaroo and snake.

614 10th Avenue SW, Calgary, Alberta 403/263-4605; www.albertaboot.com Mon–Sat 9–6, public hols 11–4 (mid-Jun to mid-Jul open until 9pm weekdays)

Brick Shirt House

Great outdoor clothing. The hats, T-shirts and sweaters make great souvenirs.

C-4227 Village Stroll, Whistler, British Columbia 604/932-5320 Daily 8am–11pm

FIRST NATIONS ART

Dorothy Grant

Beautiful First Nations clothes and artifacts in traditional Haida designs.

1656 West 75th Avenue, Vancouver, British Columbia 604/681-0201; www.dorothygrant.com

Inuit Gallery of Vancouver

Works by Inuit and First Nations artists – soapstone animal sculptures, traditional masks, jewelry, gifts.

206 Cambie Street, Vancouver, British Columbia 604/688-7323, 888/615-8399; www.inuit.com

MALLS

Metropolis at Metrotown

Around 500 stores, more than 20 movie theaters and the Entertainment Centre make this the second-largest mall in the world (after Edmonton).

4700 Kingsway, Burnaby, Vancouver, British Columbia 604/438-4700; www.metropolisatmetrotown.com

West Edmonton Mall

The world's biggest shopping mall, with more than 800 stores (➤ 73 and 159).

✉ 8882 170th Street, Edmonton, Alberta ☎ 780/444-5200; www.westedmall.com

MARKET

Granville Island Public Market

One of North America's finest food markets, with a stunning array of meat, fish, cheese, fruit, wine and specialty food stands.

✉ Johnston Street, Granville Island, Vancouver, British Columbia ☎ 604/666-5784; www.granvilleisland.bc.ca

SPECIALTY STORES

Approach at the Station

One of Vancouver's better souvenir shops; great for typical Canadian goods, some made locally, including jewelry, leather, glassware and wood.

✉ 14 - 601 Cordova Street West, Vancouver, British Columbia ☎ 604/689-0930; www.theapproachatthestation.com

Klondike Nugget and Ivory Shop

Exquisite jewelry is made here using Dawson gold nuggets – in business for more than 90 years.

✉ Front and Queen streets, Dawson City, Yukon ☎ 867/993-5432

Totem Ski Shop

Great outdoor wear, including a fine range of footwear, sweatshirts and handknit Cowichan sweaters, which make great souvenirs.

✉ 408 Connaught Drive, Jasper, Alberta ☎ 780/852-3078, 800/363-3078 (toll-free); www.totemskishop.com

Places to take the children

Beringia

This splendid interpretive center presents the Yukon as it was when woolly mammoths roamed the area 40,000 years ago, and its mammoth skeleton is a major attraction for children. They will also be thrilled by the scimitar cats and the unbelievably huge giant beavers.

✉ Mile 915 (Km1,473) Alaska Highway, south of Whitehorse International Airport, Yukon ☎ 867/667-8855; www.beringia.com 🕐 Mid-May to Sep daily 9–5; Oct to mid-May Sun 1–5 ✋ Moderate

Calaway Park

Thrills and spills for children of all ages at western Canada's largest outdoor amusement park, with rides, mini-golf, a haunted mansion and more.

✉ 254033 Range Road 33; 10km (6 miles) west of Calgary on TransCanada Highway at Springbank Road, Alberta ☎ 403/240-3822; www.calawaypark.com 🕐 Jul–early Sep daily 10–7; mid-May to Jun Fri 5–9, Sat–Sun 10–7; early Sep to mid-Oct Sat–Sun 11–6 ✋ Expensive

Calgary Zoo, Botanical Gardens and Prehistoric Park

See page 146.

Children's Maritime Discovery Centre

Educational fun for children of all ages.

✉ Vancouver Maritime Museum, 1095 Ogden Avenue, Vancouver, British Columbia ☎ 604/257-8300; www.vancouvermaritimemuseum.com 🕐 Early May–early Sep daily 10–5; early Sep–early May Tue–Sat 10–5, Sun 12–5 ✋ Moderate ⛴ False Creek Ferry

H.R. MacMillan Space Centre

This spectacular attraction offers space-related activities, including a realistic virtual voyage in a spacecraft simulator, multimedia show and planetarium.

✉ 1100 Chestnut Street, Vancouver, British Columbia ☎ 604/738-7827;

www.spacecentre.ca Daily 10–5. Closed Mon off season Expensive 2, 22 Aquabus

Manitoba Children's Museum

See page 140.

Telus World of Science

Fun for the whole family, with galleries including Mystery Avenue, DiscoveryLand, Space Place, The Body Fantastic, Star Theatre and The Greens House. Also an observatory and IMAX theater.

11211 - 142 Street, Edmonton, Alberta 780/452-9100; www.odyssium.com Jul–Aug daily 10–9; Sep–Jun Sun–Thu 10–5, Fri–Sat 10–9. IMAX theater: from 11am Expensive

Vancouver Aquarium

See pages 84–85.

Victoria Bug Zoo

Children will be in their element among some of the most incredible looking insects and other creepy-crawlies – they even get to hold some of them.

631 Courtney Street, Victoria, British Columbia 250/384-2847; www.bugzoo.bc.ca Jun–Labour Day weekend daily 9–9; Sep to mid-Jun Mon–Sat 10–5, Sun 11–5 Moderate

West Edmonton Mall

The world's largest indoor amusement park, with an indoor waterpark, and a great way to get the children excited about visiting a shopping center (➤ 71 and 159).

Exploring

Western Canada is so vast and varied that it defies generalizations. Contrasts here are extreme: the widespread plains of the Prairies and the massive peaks and glaciers of the Rocky Mountains; the gritty cowboy towns of Alberta and genteel, anglophile Victoria; the lush orchards and vineyards of Okanagan and the wastelands of the dusty Alberta Badlands and the Arctic tundra.

It's a region that emcompasses both the coldest and mildest winter temperatures in Canada, that is home to some of the newest arrivals and oldest cultures, and that contains some of Canada's most historic sites and one of its most modern cities – vibrant, beautiful Vancouver.

British Columbia and the Rockies

The Pacific province of British Columbia, Canada's third largest, is a land of extensive plateaux, myriad lakes, great rivers caught between rugged mountains, and islands lying off its much-indented coastline. Its natural splendor allows for a wealth of outdoor activities, from climbing, hiking and skiing to sailing, canoeing and fishing. Touring by bus, car or RV is easy and the roads are excellent.

When BC became part of Canada in 1871, about a quarter of the inhabitants were First Nations people. British settlers were followed by large groups of Chinese laborers who came to work in the gold mines and on the railroad. Today many Far Eastern influences add to the province's multicultural mix.

BC is separated from the rest of Canada by the Rocky Mountains, a natural barrier that it shares with Alberta. Access across this mighty patchwork of dramatic peaks, pristine forests and emerald lakes is via three mountain passes – Crowsnest, Kicking Horse and Yellowhead.

VANCOUVER

Its dazzling setting alone – ringed by the waters of the Pacific and the majestic snow-capped peaks of the Coast Mountains – makes Vancouver a must on any visit to British Columbia.

Few cities can match Canada's Gateway to the Pacific. Its busy multicultural population lends the city a cosmopolitan air, and together with great shopping and wonderful restaurants, outstanding museums and galleries, a vast range of recreational activities, a buzzing nightlife, green parks and fabulous views, you'll be hard pressed to know where to start.

Canada Place makes a stunning introduction to Vancouver, with sensational views of the city's port. Downtown occupies a wonderful natural setting on the south shore of Burrard Inlet, with the Strait of Georgia just offshore; its attractions cover a small area and are easily walkable. Granville Island, with its fabulous market, buzzes with life, especially on weekends, and Chinatown bursts with sights, sounds and smells, while Gastown, the redeveloped heart of Vancouver, is a dynamic mix of bars, restaurants and stores. Commercial Drive, north of Broadway, is the city's traditional Little Italy district, and residential North Shore has some of the country's most expensive real estate. And when you need to unwind, Stanley Park is the perfect place to balance the excitement that comes with any city visit.

www.tourismvancouver.com

15L

200 Burrard Street, Plaza Level 604/683-2000 Daily 8:30–6. Satellite Visitor Centre, Vancouver Art Gallery Plaza, Robin Street; hours vary seasonally

Canada Place

For the best view of Vancouver's spectacular natural setting, visit Canada Place. This waterfront building with its five vast "sails" is one of the most distinctive features on the Vancouver skyline. A stroll along the promenade comes with sensational views of skyscrapers, surrounding mountains and the cruise ship terminal, where some of the world's most luxurious vessels dock. There is an equally good viewpoint a short walk away at the Harbour Centre Building, where all-glass SkyLifts whisk you up to **The Vancouver Lookout!**, a circular observation deck.

www.canadaplace.ca; **www.**vancouverlookout.com

Vancouver 7b 100–999 Canada Place Way 604/775-7200; IMAX theater 604/682-4629 Daily 4, 7, 17 on Burrard; 4, 7, 50 on Granville SkyTrain: Waterfront Free; IMAX: expensive

The Vancouver Lookout!

555 West Hastings Street 604/689-0421 May to mid-Oct daily 8:30–10:30; mid-Oct to Apr 9–9 Expensive 4, 19, 22, 44 on Robson

Chinatown

North America's third-largest Chinatown (after San Francisco and New York) dates from around 1858 when Chinese immigrants flocked here during the Fraser Valley Gold Rush. Many more came to work on the trans-continental railroad in the 1880s and others came in the 1990s, before Hong Kong was handed back to China. Today this fascinating district is crammed with tiny, crowded streets and alleys, vibrant markets and stores filled with oriental food and ancient herbal remedies. You can buy almost anything at the night market (Friday–Sun evenings 6–11pm). Take in some of the exotic stores and restaurants, then visit the **Dr. Sun Yat-Sen Classical Chinese Garden,** named for the founder of the Chinese Republic, who was a regular visitor to Vancouver. A harmonious blend of plantings and space, the gardens were created in classical Chinese style.

Vancouver 8c Along East Pender, Abbot and Keefer streets and Gore Avenue 19, 22 east on Pender Street

Dr. Sun-Yat Sen Classical Chinese Garden

578 Carrall Street 604/662-3207; www.vancouverchinesegarden.com May to mid-Jun, Sep daily 10–6; mid-Jun to Aug daily 9:30–7; Oct daily 10–4:30; Nov–Apr Tue–Sun 10–4:30 Moderate Café ($) 19, 22

Granville Island

Granville Island is one of Vancouver's most vibrant cultural and commercial centers. This former swampland has been transformed into an attractive riverside area. Connected to downtown by the Granville Street Bridge, it is a thriving medley of stores, restaurants, galleries, artists' studios, nightclubs and one of the world's greatest **food markets.** In addition to the wonderful bustling food market, there's **Granville Island Brewing,** which offers guided tours and tastings, and a trio of **museums** under one roof featuring sport fishing, model ships and model trains.

Vancouver 3f

Granville Island Infocentre

1398 Cartwright Street 604/666-5784; www.granvilleisland.bc.ca
Many cafés, bars and restaurants ($–$$$) 50 Downtown Historic Railway from Science Centre (May to mid-Oct 1–5)

Food Market

1689 Johnston Street Daily 9–6. Closed Mon in winter

Granville Island Brewing

1441 Cartwright Street 604/687-2739; www.gib.ca Tours daily

Granville Island Museums

1502 Duranleau Street 604/683-1939; www.sportfishingmuseum.ca
Tue–Sun 10–5:30 Moderate

Maritime Museum

Take the water taxi from Granville Island to Vanier Park, where the Maritime Museum explores Vancouver's strong ties with the sea. Pride of place goes to the *St Roch*, a two-masted Royal Canadian Mounted Police schooner, built in the 1920s. In 1944 it became the first vessel to sail through the treacherous Northwest Passage between Baffin Island and Alaska's Beaufort Sea. There is also a section about pirates and the Children's Maritime Discovery Centre (➤ 72).

www.vancouvermaritimemusuem.com

✚ *Vancouver 1d* ✉ 1095 Ogden Avenue ☎ 604/257-8300 🕐 May–early Sep daily 10–5; early Sep–Apr Tue–Sat 10–5, Sun 12–5 Moderate 🚌 2, 22 ⛴ Water taxi from Granville Island

Museum of Anthropology

Best places to see, ➤ 48–49.

North Shore

Vancouver's North Shore – comprising the District of West Vancouver and the District and City of North Vancouver – lies across Burrard Inlet and English Bay, backed by Grouse Mountain, Capilano Regional Park, Lighthouse Park, and the Cypress, Lyn Canyon and Mount Seymour provincial parks.

Access to the exclusive residential area of West Vancouver is via the Lion's Gate Bridge and to North Vancouver by SeaBus from the terminal near Canada Place (➤ 79). Lonsdale Quay in North Vancouver has great shopping, including a fine indoor market, and you can watch the ships come and go from the observation tower or nearby Waterfront Park.

Cypress, Grouse and Seymour mountains dominate the scene, but the highlight is Grouse Mountain. Here you go to the top by cable-car, where the Theatre in the Sky gives panoramic views of Vancouver and its surroundings. Below Grouse Mountain, Capilano Gorge has the world's oldest (1889) and longest (137m/450ft) suspension footbridge (entrance fee), 76m (250ft) above the river.

Vancouver 8a (off map)

North Shore Tourism

102–124 West 1st Street, North Vancouver 604/987-4488; www.nvchamber.bc.ca Range of eateries along North Shore ($–$$$) N24, 242 SeaBus to North Vancouver

Capilano Suspension Bridge

3735 Capilano Road, North Vancouver 604/985-7474; www.capbridge.com May–Sep daily 8:30/9–7/8/9; Sep–early Dec daily 9–5/6/7; early Dec–early Jan daily 10–9 (closed Christmas Day); early Jan–Apr daily 9–5/6 Expensive

Grouse Mountain Cable Car

6400 Nancy Greene Way, North Vancouver 604/984-0661; www.grousemountain.com Daily 9am–10pm Expensive 236 from Lonsdale Quay, 232 from Phibbs Exchange

Stanley Park

Best places to see, ➤ 54–55.

Telus World of Science

The futuristic geodesic dome at the eastern end of False Creek, built for Expo '86, has become a distinctive Vancouver landmark. Here the mysteries of science are unraveled in a lively and entertaining way, with daily demonstrations at the ground level center stage and hands-on interactive displays. In addition to the Sara Stern Gallery, Eureka, KidSpace, Our World and Visual Illusions, there is a Special Exhibitions Gallery and a science theater. The OMNIMAX theater on the upper level shows the latest blockbuster movies on one of the largest dome screens in the world.

www.scienceworld.ca

Vancouver 8e 1455 Québec Street 604/443-7440, 604/443-7443 (24-hour information) Mon–Fri 10–5, Sat–Sun 10–6 White Spot Triple O ($) Expensive 3, 8 north on Granville Mall, 19 on Pender Street SkyTrain Millennium Line to Science World–Main Street, Expo Line to King George False Creek Ferry

Vancouver Aquarium

Stanley Park (➤ 54–55) is home to the Vancouver Aquarium, probably the city's, and Canada's, most popular attraction. Inside are more than 8,000 aquatic creatures, representing over 600

different marine species, with the emphasis on those from the Northwest and the Arctic. In 2006, to celebrate its 50th anniversary, the aquarium opened an impressive new Discover Education Centre, plus various extended and reorganized exhibits within the existing areas.

It's hard not to be impressed by the re-creations of a humid Amazon rain forest with giant sloths, iguanas, brightly colored tropical birds and crocodiles, and an Indonesian coral reef, complete with angelfish and blacktip reef sharks, but for most people the big draws are the performing dolphins and the whales. The Arctic Canada habitat gives you the chance to see beluga whales close up through huge underwater windows. Although these graceful creatures are well cared for, there has been concern from animal rights groups about keeping large sea mammals in captivity. It remains an ongoing issue, although the aquarium authorities are working hard at promoting a conservation agenda.

Children enjoy the tidal pools, where they can touch anemones and starfish. Also popular are the delightful antics of the sea otters, sea lions and harbor seals.

www.vanaqua.org

Vancouver 1a (off map) 845 Avison Way, Stanley Park 604/659-3474 Late Jun–early Sep daily 9:30–7; early Sep–late Jun daily 9:30–5. Call ahead for feeding times Expensive Upstream Café ($) 19, 135, Express Bus

Vancouver Art Gallery

A former 1911 city courthouse has been transformed into downtown's principal sight, the Vancouver Art Gallery. The gallery holds over 9,000 works in its permanent collection, reflecting a remarkable record of British Columbian art. It owns the largest collection of works by BC's most acclaimed artist, Emily Carr, some of which are usually on display.

The gallery also features works by Dutch, French, Italian, German and English masters, sculpture, graphics, video works and an extensive photographic collection, and presents touring historical and contemporary exhibitions. These latter exhibitions feature prominently, and works by modern international artists can often be dramatic and challenging.

The neoclassical building, a work of art in its own right, was redesigned in the 1980s by Arthur Erickson and makes a wonderful setting for the art. The attractive café, with its delightful patio roof, serves excellent coffee, snacks and light meals and the gallery shop has a fine range of handcrafted items. Plans are under way for a new venue for the gallery in a waterside setting on False Creek's Plaza of Nations.

www.vanartgallery.bc.ca

Vancouver 5c 750 Hornby Street 604/662-4719 Daily 10–5:30 (also Tue and Thu 5:30–9 Expensive Gallery Café ($–$$) 5, 15 Burrard or Granville

Vancouver Museum

In 1968 Canada's largest civic museum moved to its present location in a futuristic building designed by Gerald Hamilton. Its extensive collections – hundred of thousands of specimens and artifacts – do an excellent job of tracing the history of Vancouver and the First Nations.

The museum has current plans for repositioning its content and curatorial role towards a greater focus on Vancouver in a modern context. Plans include a potential move to the heart of downtown, with the current Vancouver Art Gallery building on Hornby Street being considered when it is vacated (► opposite).

The H.R. MacMillan Space Centre (► 72–73) adjoins the museum. Here, among other things, you can take a virtual trip to Mars or try to design a spacecraft.

www.vanmuseum.bc.ca

Vancouver 1d 1100 Chestnut Street, Vanier Park 604/736-4431 Daily 10–5 (also Thu 5–9). Closed Mon Sep–Jun and Dec 25 Moderate Vending machines ($) 2, 22

More to see in British Columbia and the Rockies

ALASKA HIGHWAY

One of the world's great adventures, the Alaska Highway recalls the intrepid journeys of old in North America's northern frontiers. Today's highway is a far cry from the original route that was laid out through mosquito-infested swampland in 1942 as a military access road. It ran for 2,446km (1,520 miles), winding its way from Dawson Creek in British Columbia to Fairbanks in Alaska (U.S.A.). Although it officially ends at Delta Junction, most people continue to Fairbanks, 158km (98 miles) farther.

Also known as the Alcan Highway, it begins as Highway 97 in Dawson Creek, traditionally at the Mile Zero cairn. Fort St. John (Mile 47) is the oldest European settlement on mainland British Columbia, and Stone Mountain Provincial Park (Mile 392) has the highest point on the road at Summit Lake (1,378m/4,521ft). Laird Hot Springs (Mile 496) rank among the finest natural hot springs in Canada. The pools here have an average temperature of 46°C (115°F) and are surrounded by a lush floral carpet, including many species of orchid.

From here it's another 224km (139 miles) to Watson Lake (Mile

635), the Yukon's first town (➤ 174). The highway crosses the Yukon border several times between Mile 588 and 627, the official crossing. At Watson Lake the Campbell Highway swings north and west and runs parallel to the Alaska Highway through eastern Yukon, ending at Carmacks.

The highway is accessible year round, weather permitting. If you plan to drive the whole route, remember it involves crossing the U.S. border, so take the necessary documents and currency.

16G

Dawson Creek Visitor Information Centre, Station Museum, 900 Alaska Avenue, Dawson Creek, British Columbia, 250/782-9595; www.tourismdawsoncreek.com, May–Aug daily 8–5:30; Sep–Apr Tue–Sat 10–5

Fort St. John Visitor Information Centre, 9523 100th Street, Fort St. John, British Columbia, 250/785-3033, May–Aug Mon–Fri 8–7, Sat–Sun 9–6; Sep–Apr Mon–Fri 9–5

BANFF

Banff's superb location – at 1,383m (4,537ft), it's the highest town in Canada – its excellent visitor center and its attractions make it an obvious base for exploring Banff National Park (► 36–37). The **Whyte Museum of the Canadian Rockies,** portraying local life and landscapes with paintings, photographs and artifacts, is worth a visit. The Sulphur Mountain Gondola, 3km (2 miles) south of town on Mountain Avenue, has a daily cable-car ride (expensive) up to Canada's highest restaurant for fine views, while the **Cave and Basin National Historic Site,** to the southeast, is an interpretive center based around the hot springs discovered in 1883. If you want to take a dip, you'll need to head instead for **Upper Hot Springs,** a modern complex where the sulfurous waters emerge at a steamy 42°C (108°F).

17L

Banff Information Centre 224 Banff Avenue, Banff, Alberta 403/762-1550; www.pc.gc.ca/pn-np/ab/banff Mid-May to late Jun daily 9–7; late Jun to mid-Sep daily 8–8; mid-Sep to mid-May daily 9–5

Whyte Museum of the Canadian Rockies

✉ 111 Bear Street ☎ 403/762-2291 ⏲ Daily 10–5 ✋ Moderate

Cave and Basin National Historic Site

✉ 311 Cave Avenue ☎ 403/762-1566 ⏲ Mid-May to Sep daily 9–6; Oct to mid-May Mon–Fri 11–4, Sat–Sun 9:30–5 ✋ Inexpensive

Upper Hot Springs

✉ Mountain Avenue, 4km (2.5 miles) south of Banff ☎ 403/762-1515 ⏲ Mid-May to early Sep daily 9am–11pm; early Sep to mid-May 10–10 (also 10–11pm Fri–Sat) ✋ Moderate

BANFF NATIONAL PARK

Best places to see, ➤ 36–37.

CARIBOO CHILCOTIN

This vast range stretches from the fjords of the Pacific Coast across British Columbia's interior plateau to the foothills of the Cariboo Mountains. It is gold and cattle country, with vast forests, a deeply indented coastline, small fishing villages and coastal rain forests. It has some of the world's largest cattle ranches and much of BC's best freshwater fishing. Bella Coola, a sport angler's dream, is where the Bella Coola River joins the Pacific, at the end of Highway 20 from Williams Lake. The Cariboo Highway, from Williams Lake to Quesnel, is the heart of the area.

Quesnel, north of Williams Lake, was built in the 1860s at the confluence of the Fraser and Quesnel rivers. From here prospectors traveled to the local gold fields. Today tourists follow, to visit the reconstructed Gold Rush town of **Barkerville.**

✚ 15J

ℹ North Cariboo Tourism ✉ 339A Reid Street, Quesnel, British Columbia ☎ 205/992-3522; www.northcariboo.com

Barkerville Historic Town

✉ PO Box 19, Barkerville, British Columbia ☎ 888/994-3332; www.barkerville.ca ⏲ Late May–Sep daily 8–8 ✋ Expensive

FRASER CANYON AND HELL'S GATE

In 1808 American-born fur trader Simon Fraser led an expedition in canoes down what he thought was the Columbia River. It wasn't, and the river now bears his name. Rising in Mount Robson National Park, the Fraser, one of Canada's great waterways, flows 1,279km (795 miles) southwest to the Pacific. About 48km (30 miles) south of Lytton is Hell's Gate, nature at its most magnificent. Here the Fraser Canyon, 183m (600ft) deep and just 30m (98ft) wide, forces the river into a narrow channel, and at peak spring levels water equaling twice the volume of Niagara Falls surges through here.

The **Hell's Gate AirTram** cable-car descends into the gorge to a suspension bridge and observation deck for views of the river below. In 1913 a landslide during construction of the Canadian Pacific Railway wiped out millions of salmon. It wasn't until 1945 that fish ladders were built to enable them to bypass the gorge.

✚ 15L

Hell's Gate AirTram

✉ Hell's Gate, 9.6km (6 miles) north of Yale, British Columbia ☎ 604/867-9277 ⌚ Mid-Apr to mid-May, early Sep–Oct daily 10–4; mid-May to early Sep daily 10–5 Expensive Café ($), Salmon House Restaurant ($–$$)

GLACIER AND MOUNT REVELSTOKE NATIONAL PARKS

The mountains immediately to the west of the Rockies are every bit as spectacular as the Rockies themselves, and parts are protected by these two small adjoining national parks. Glacier National Park, the larger of the two, remained virtually uninhabited until the Canadian Pacific Railway was driven through in 1885 via Rogers Pass. Visitors flocked to the pass's hotel, but the line closed in 1916 when the Connaught tunnel opened, and tourist numbers only recovered when the TransCanada Highway opened. Some 14 percent of the park is permanently under snow, and has more than 420 glaciers, while the rest is a feast of stunning scenery. The Rogers Pass Visitor Centre has details of walks.

To the west, Mount Revelstoke National Park was created in 1914 to protect the mountain's alpine meadows. The main access is on the 26km (16-mile) Meadows in the Sky Parkway, near the town of Revelstoke. The aptly named parkway climbs toward the summit of Mount Revelstoke (1,938m/6,358ft) where there are walks and hikes, and places to enjoy the view or have a picnic.

✚ 17K

ℹ Rogers Pass Visitor Centre, British Columbia ☎ 250/837-7500; www.pc.gc.ca/pn-np/bc/revelstoke or /glacier ⌚ Mid-Jun to Aug daily 7:30am–8pm; May to mid-Jun, Sep–Oct daily 8:30–4:30; Nov Thu–Mon 8:30–4:30; Dec–Apr daily 7–5

HOWE SOUND

Best places to see, ➤ 40–41.

ICEFIELDS PARKWAY

Best places to see, ➤ 42–43.

JASPER

Jasper is the main town in Jasper National Park (➤ 44–45), the largest preserved wilderness area in the Rocky Mountains. The park visitor center is a natural historic site in an attractive garden setting and a gathering place for visitors. The main attraction in town is the **Yellowhead Museum and Archives,** with modest displays that highlight the town's history and its role in the fur trade. It also has a small art gallery.

The **Jasper Tramway,** a cable-car 7km (4.3 miles) south of town, takes visitors up 2,277m (7,472ft) on Whistler Mountain. It's busy in summer so arrive early, but it's worth the wait for the views. There's also a restaurant, interpretive center and a trail that continues up the mountain for even more impressive panoramas.

17K

Jasper Visitor Information 500 Connaught Drive, Jasper, Alberta 780/852-6176; www.pc.gc.ca/jasper

Yellowhead Museum and Archives

400 Pyramid Avenue 780/852-3013; www.jaspermuseum.org May–Sep daily 10–5; Oct–Apr Thu–Sun 10–5 Inexpensive

Jasper Tramway

Whistler Mountain Road 780/852-3093, 866/850-8726 (toll-free); www.jaspertramway.com Late Jun–late Aug daily 9–8; mid-Apr to mid-May, late Aug–early Oct daily 10–5; mid-May to late Jun daily 9:30–6:30 Expensive Treeline Restaurant ($$)

JASPER NATIONAL PARK

Best places to see, ➤ 44–45.

KOOTENAY NATIONAL PARK

Kootenay is the least visited of the four Rocky Mountain national parks, but its jagged peaks and river-cut forests are as impressive as any in Canada. The park is bisected by the Banff–Windermere Parkway (Highway 93), linking all the major attractions. It enters from the east at Castle Junction. About 8km (5 miles) from here is Vermilion Pass (1,651m/5,417ft), marking the Continental Divide, from where rivers flow west to the Pacific and east to the Atlantic. About 3km (1.8 miles) south of Vermilion Pass is the starting point for the Glacier Trail to a superb view of Stanley Glacier and the Hanging Valley below Stanley Peak.

Marble Canyon, a 37m (121ft) deep gorge 8km (5 miles) south of Vermilion Pass, is the main point of interest. The chemical composition of its rock creates a wide range of colors. A short trail follows the gorge to a thunderous waterfall, and can be combined with the trail to the Paint Pots, iron-rich mineral springs that bubble up and stain the water and earth orange-yellow. The highway exits the park near Radium Hot Springs (Canada's largest) at the base of dramatic Sinclair Canyon.

17L

Park Visitor Centre 7556 Main Street East, Radium Hot Springs, British Columbia 250/347-9505; www.pc.gc.ca/kootenay Late Jun–early Sep daily 9–7; late May–late Jun, early Sep to mid-Oct daily 9–5 Moderate

Kootenay Park Lodge Visitor Centre 68km (42 miles) north of Radium Hot Springs on Highway 93 at Vermillion Crossing Jul–Aug daily 9–6; late May–Jun, Sep daily 10–5. Closed Oct–late May

a walk to Lake Agnes

Park in the Lake Louise parking lot and make your way to the lakeshore promenade for exceptional water level views of the landscape and the Château Lake Louise hotel.

With the water on your left, walk along the lakefront until the footpath splits. Take the right-hand fork climbing immediately from the water's edge.

After 1.2km (0.7 miles) a fine view of the lake appears on the left (from above the waterline the incredible blue tone is even more apparent).

The route takes a tight dog-leg here and soon reaches a junction with a horse track coming in from the right. Keep left.

The path reaches a plateau after 1.9km (1.1 miles), where you can stop and admire Mirror Lake, backed by a wall of rock and surrounded by shady trees.

Take the footpath right from the lake.

Enjoy the views east across the broad sweep of Bow Valley.

The path then swings left, before the final climb to Lake Agnes, a steep flight of steps to the right of a rock wall.

Once you've climbed the steps you will see Lake Agnes's pretty setting, with a curtain of peaks on all sides and the Big Beehive rock formation to your left. The famous Tea House serves sandwiches, soup, cakes and, of course, tea. You may have to wait a while during frequent busy periods.

Return the way you came.

For a longer hike, follow the north side of the lake and then up steep zig-zags to a saddle. Go left to the top of the Big Beehive. Return to the saddle and go left down the continuation path. Turn left at the next junction to return to Lake Louise via Mirror Lake (additional 6km/3.8 miles).

Distance 4km (2.5 miles)
Time 2 hours
Start point Lake Louise Car Park ✚ 17K
End point Lake Agnes Tea House
Lunch Lake Agnes Tea House ($–$$) ☎ 403/522-3511 (Château Lake Louise Hotel, which operates it) 🕒 Jun to mid-Oct daily 9–6

LAKE LOUISE AND MORAINE LAKE

Few sights can compare to Lake Louise, a peerless body of water hidden in the mountains. This sapphire lake, backed by mountains, glaciers and tumbling forests, was named in honor of Queen Victoria's daughter, Princess Louise Caroline Alberta, who was married to the Governor General of Canada. The world-famous Fairmont Château Lake Louise Hotel (➤ 107), begun in 1890, dominates its eastern shore. Vivid turquoise waters are the main focus, and there are soaring mountains all around.

There's a broad, open area in front of the hotel that gives a superb view over the lake toward the mountains. You'll get a better view from the **Lake Louise Gondola,** a cable-car that runs up Mount Whitehorn (2,668m/8,753ft). There is an excellent visitor center in Lake Louise Village, 5km (3 miles) before Lake Louise.

Fewer people visit Moraine Lake, 13km (8 miles) south of Lake Louise on Moraine Lake Road, but it's equally beautiful. The "Jewel of the Rockies" lies at the foot of the stupendous snow-dusted Wenkchemna Mountains. (This scene used to appear on the Canadian $20 bill.) The best stroll is along the lakeshore; the best walk is to Consolation Lake, 3.2km (2 miles) away.

17K Station Restaurant at Lake Louise (➤ 108–109)

Visitor Centre Next to Samson Mall, Lake Louise Village, Alberta 403/522-3833; www.pc.gc.ca/pn-np/ab/banff Late Jun to mid-Sep daily 9–7/8; mid-Sep to late Jun daily 9–4/5

Lake Louise Gondola

Off Whitehorn Road 403/522-3555 Jun–Sep daily 9–4 (8:30–6 Jun, Sep) Lodge of the Ten Peaks ($), summer 7:30am–6pm

OKANAGAN VALLEY

This region of low hills, peaceful lakes and pastoral countryside centers on the towns of Vernon, Kelowna and Penticton, ranged north to south along Okanagan Lake. Its mild, almost Mediterranean climate is perfect for fruit growing, which accounts for the vineyards and orchards. Many of the wineries offer tours and tastings and can be visited by following the Okanagan Wine Route. The **British Columbia Wine Information Centre** at Penticton has information.

Kelowna is the hub of activity. Its name derives from the First Nations word for grizzly bear, which, in fact, referred to the grizzled appearance of an early settler. The town's location midway along the lakeshore gives it access to a range of watersports, from windsurfing to parasailing. Equipment and boats can be rented.

Eleven kilometers (7 miles) north of Vernon is the **Historic O'Keefe Ranch,** a collection of original pioneer buildings and a museum that give a taste of ranching life in the 19th century.

16L

Thompson Okanagan Tourism Association 2280-D Leckie Road, Kelowna, British Columbia 250/860-5999, 800/567-2275 (toll-free); www.totabc.com

British Columbia Wine Information Centre
553 Railway Street, Penticton, British Columbia
250/490-2006; www.bcwineinfo.ca

Historic O'Keefe Ranch
9380 Highway 97 North, Vernon, British Columbia
250/542-7868; www.okeeferanch.ca May–late Oct daily 9–6 (Jul–Aug to 8pm) Moderate

WATERTON LAKES NATIONAL PARK

First established in 1895, Waterton Lakes National Park, with its unusual geology, rare wild flowers and abundant wildlife, is today recognized as a biosphere reserve. Rising abruptly out of the prairies, this rare gem protects 521sq km (200sq miles) of the Canadian Rockies in Southwest Alberta, close to the U.S. border. Choose from a wide range of sporting possibilities or over 160km (100 miles) of trails, with opportunities for day and half-day hikes from Waterton townsite. A popular excursion is to walk across the U.S. border (documentation needed) on the Waterton Lakeshore Trail (13km/8 miles) to Goat Haunt in Montana's Glacier National Park. Two specially built scenic roads, the Akamina Parkway (20km/ 12 miles) and the Red Rock Canyon Parkway (14km/8.5 miles), which leads through a dramatic 20m (66ft) deep iron-red gorge, are both accessed from close to Waterton.The highlight of the park's chain of sparkling lakes, carved out of the rock by ancient glaciers, is Upper Waterton Lake; at close to 150m (492ft) it's the deepest in the Canadian Rockies.

18M Cafés and restaurants in Waterton townsite ($–$$$)
Park Administrative Office Box 200 Waterton Park, Waterton, Alberta 403/859-2224; www.pc.gc.ca/pn-np/ab/waterton Daily; Visitor Centre mid-May to mid-Oct Moderate

WELLS GRAY PROVINCIAL PARK

Wells Gray is one of the finest of BC's mountain parks, although it is less visibly rugged and mountainous than the mighty peaks of Jasper and Banff. Access begins at Clearwater where a 60km (37-mile) road enters and heads north, passing viewpoints, waterfalls, rivers and forests. Most sights are accessed from this road.

About 8km (5 miles) from Clearwater, just after the main road crosses the park boundary, a short trail leads via a winding side road to 61m (200ft) Spahats Falls, with its brightly colored layers of pink-gray volcanic rock. Green Mountain Lookout has sensational views of the whole park. Dawson Falls is a powerful, short but wide cascade, and farther along is Helmcken Falls. At over twice the height of Niagara Falls, this is the park's centerpiece. Here the water cascades into a deep-cut, tree-fringed bowl in a single graceful plume. The park offers great hiking in summer and skiing in winter, but virtually no services, so fill up with gas and take enough picnic supplies.

16K Clearwater ($–$$$) Clearwater Visitor Infocentre 425 E Yellowhead Highway (Highway 5), British Columbia 250/674-2646; www.wellsgray.ca Jun–Aug daily 9–7; Sep–May 9–4 Visitor Centre free; park inexpensive

a drive around Icefields Parkway

This magnificent drive between Lake Louise and Jasper takes you through some of the most majestic scenery in the Rockies (➤ 42–43).

Take Route 1 north, then the right exit for Route 93 (Icefields Parkway), just north of Lake Louise village (stop at the ticket office in 2km/1.2 miles for a park pass if you don't already have one).

You'll pass tiny Hector Lake soon after the ticket office, but the first important landmark is Crowfoot Glacier, off to the left, 34km (21 miles) from Lake Louise.

About 6.4km (4 miles) farther is a left turn to Peyto Lake Lookout (➤ 51).

From the parking area it is an easy 20-minute stroll to one of the most breathtaking viewpoints in the Rockies.

After 72km (45 miles) there is parking for Mistaya Canyon. In another 5km (3 miles) you will reach Saskatchewan River Crossing.

Here you can get refreshments, accommodations and the last gas until Jasper.

The parkway follows the North Saskatchewan River, with jagged peaks on either side.

Cirrus Mountain is on the right (parking on the left) before you reach a huge curve in the road. From the parking lot at the top you get a great view down the valley. The 2.5km (1.5-mile) steep walk along Parker Ridge leads to great views of the Saskatchewan Glacier.

Past Parker Ridge cross from Banff National Park into Jasper National Park. Nearly 10km (6 miles) later you reach the Columbia Icefield Centre, where you can get glacier trips. The Icefield Centre has several exhibitions, shopping and a large café-restaurant.

At North Columbia Icefield the mountains recede a little as the road follows the wider flood plain of the Sunwapta River. Look for Sunwapta Falls and Athabasca Falls.

From Athabasca Falls it's 29km (18 miles) to Jasper *(► 94).*

Distance 230km (143 miles)
Time One day, two if you include longer walks and the Athabasca Glacier trip
Start point Lake Louise village 17K
End point Jasper 17K
Lunch Icefield Centre, or stock up with food and drink for a picnic

WHISTLER

Whistler lies 123km (76 miles) north of Vancouver amid stunning mountain scenery and is one of North America's finest ski destinations. Non-skiers can experience the thrill in a chauffeured ski-chair, the SNO-LIMO. Whistler is to host the Winter Olympic Games in 2010.

This weekend playground for Vancouverites, nestling between the peaks of Whistler and Blackcomb mountains, is only two-and-a-half hours from the city on the scenic Sea to Sky Highway or the scenic train ride, the **Whistler Mountaineer.** It has a range of summer activities too, including golf, mountain biking, fishing, rollerblading, ziplining and even skiing on Blackcomb's Horstmann Glacier. Garibaldi Provincial Park, just south, draws hikers and mountain bikers.

15K Several departures daily from Vancouver and Vancouver airport

Float (sea) planes from Vancouver

Whistler Visitor Centre 4230 Gateway Drive, Whistler, British Columbia 604/935-3357 Daily 8–8

Whistler Mountaineer

Pacific Central Station, 100–1150 Station Street, Vancouver, British Columbia 604/606-8460, 888/687-7245 (toll-free); www.whistlermountaineer.com Downtown bus pick-up 7:15–7:45am; train departs North Vancouver station 8:30am, arrives Whistler 11:30am. Departs Whistler station 3pm, arrives North Vancouver station 6pm Expensive Breakfast and afternoon tea included

YOHO NATIONAL PARK

This stunning park with its snow-topped mountains, spectacular waterfalls and roaring rivers deserves its name – Yoho is Cree for "awesome." It is bisected by the scenic TransCanada Highway, which climbs parallel to the railroad from Alberta to the BC boundary at Kicking Horse Pass (1,625m/5,330ft). At the heart of Yoho is Field, the park's only settlement, and two side roads close by give access to some of the park's best trails.

The major draws are the lakes, waterfalls and the Spiral Tunnels. Emerald Lake has one of the prettiest vistas anywhere in the park and is perfect for canoeing. About 8km (5 miles) east of Field are the Spiral Tunnels, a pair of figure-eight tunnels that curl around to relieve the steep gradient. People gather to watch the front of incredibly long freight trains emerging from one part of the mountain while the rear has still to enter the tunnel.

On the slopes of Mount Dennis are the famous 530-million-year-old Burgess Shales fossil beds, which have yielded the petrified remains of around 170 species of soft-bodied creatures. Access is restricted – contact the visitor center for details.

At 381m (1,250ft), Takakkaw Falls, fed by the meltwaters of the Waputik Icefield, are some of the highest highway-accessible falls in North America, dropping in a series of magnificent cascades.

17K Emerald Lake Lodge ($–$$$)

Yoho Visitor Centre Highway 1, 1.5km (1 mile) east of Field, British Columbia 250/343-6783; www.pc.gc.ca/yoho Late Jun–early Sep daily 9–7; early May–late Jun, early Sep to mid-Sep daily 9–5; Oct–Apr daily 9–4

HOTELS

BANFF, ALBERTA

Fairmont Banff Springs ($$$$)

This huge Gothic building is one of North America's most famous hotels. It's some distance from downtown, but rooms are luxurious and the amenities excellent – including the spa.

405 Spray Avenue 403/762-2211, 866/540-4406 (reservations, toll-free); www.fairmont.com/banffsprings

Juniper Hotel ($$–$$$)

Located 2km (1.5 miles) from the center of Banff, this stylish, comfortable hotel has superb views and the chalet-type rooms are beautifully appointed. The Juniper (Muk-a-Muk) Bistro is on site (► 108).

1 Juniper Way (Mount Norquay Road) 403/762-2281, 866/551-2281 (toll-free); www.thejuniper.com

ICEFIELDS PARKWAY, ALBERTA

Columbia Icefield Chalet ($$–$$$)

A reasonable place to stop between Banff and Jasper. At least half the rooms have spectacular views of the Athabasca Glacier.

PO Box 1140, Banff; on Icefields Parkway, border of Banff/Jasper national parks 403/762-6700, 877/423-7433 (toll-free) Closed early Oct–Apr

JASPER, ALBERTA

Fairmont Jasper Park Lodge ($$$$)

Jasper's equivalent of the Fairmont Banff Springs is 5km (3 miles) out of town on Lac Beauvert, amid spectacular scenery. It has rustic or modern-style rooms, a golf course, tennis courts and heated outdoor pool.

PO Box 40, Old Lodge Road 780/852-3301, 866/540-4454 (reservations, toll-free); www.fairmont.com/jasper

KELOWNA, BRITISH COLUMBIA

Lake Okanagan Resort ($$–$$$$)

A beautiful lakeside resort about 17km (10.5 miles) from Kelowna, amid 121ha (300 acres) of wooded parkland. Most rooms are on

the lakeshore. It has a par-3 golf course, two outdoor pools, tennis courts, marina and beach.
✉ 2751 Westside Road ☎ 250/769-3511, 800/663-3273 (toll-free in North America); www.lakeokanagan.com

LAKE LOUISE, ALBERTA

Fairmont Château Lake Louise ($$$)

This famous hotel overlooks beautiful Lake Louise and the Victoria Glacier, and some rooms have private terraces. All meals and activities are included in the rates. The downside is that the area around the hotel frequently gets crowded with day visitors.
✉ Lake Louise Drive ☎ 403/522-3511; www.fairmont.com/lakelouise

VANCOUVER, BRITISH COLUMBIA

Four Seasons ($$$$)

The luxurious hotel is at the heart of the shopping and financial districts. Rooms are small, but deluxe rooms and suites are available. The health club, pool and fitness center are first class.
✉ 791 West Georgia Street ☎ 604/689-9333, 800/268-6282 (toll-free in Canada), 800/819-5053 (reservations, toll free); www.fourseasons.com

Listel Hotel ($$–$$$)

An attractive boutique hotel with style, in everything from amenities to artwork. The Listel is at the heart of Westend Vancouver. There are various culture-themed package deals.
✉ 130 Robson Street ☎ 604/684-8461; www.thelistelhotel.com

WHISTLER, BRITISH COLUMBIA

Westin Resort and Spa ($$$$)

Spectacular mountain views, excellent leisure amenities and superb cuisine are on offer here. The suites have modern furnishings and the spa is one of Canada's finest.
✉ 4090 Whistler Way ☎ 604/905-5000, 888/634-5577 (toll-free); www.westinwhistler.com

RESTAURANTS

BANFF, ALBERTA

💎💎 Juniper Bistro and Lounge ($$)

Known also as Muk-a-Muk (the Chinook word for feast), this hotel-linked eatery has superb views to go with such treats as tomato soup with organic gin, seafood hotpot and bison short ribs.

✉ Juniper Hotel, 1 Juniper Way ☎ 403/762-2281, 877/762-2281 (toll-free) 🕒 Breakfast, lunch and dinner daily

💎💎💎 Le Beaujolais ($$$)

The elegant interior is wood paneled, the tables covered in crisp white linen, and the food thoroughly French. You can eat à la carte, or choose from one of the set-price menus. There is an extensive wine list.

✉ 212 Banff Avenue, corner of Buffalo Street ☎ 403/762-2712; www.lebeaujolaisbanff.com 🕒 Daily 6–9:30pm

JASPER, ALBERTA

💎💎 Villa Caruso ($–$$)

A long-time favorite serving beef, seafood and pasta. Pizzas and other dishes are made in a wood-fired oven, and the steaks are cooked in an open kitchen over a flame grill. Great views.

✉ 2nd Floor, 640 Connaught Drive ☎ 780/852-3920 🕒 Daily 11am–midnight (3–11pm off season); lunch only weekends and public hols

KELOWNA, BRITISH COLUMBIA

💎💎💎 Ric's Grill ($$)

One of a national chain of popular steak and seafood eateries, Ric's offers a good menu of traditional meat and fish dishes with international touches; also pastas, stir-fry, burgers and sandwiches.

✉ 210 Lawrence Avenue ☎ 250/869-1586; www.ricsgrill.com 🕒 Lunch Mon–Fri, dinner Sat–Sun

LAKE LOUISE, ALBERTA

💎💎 Station Restaurant at Lake Louise ($$–$$$)

Housed in the beautifully restored 1909 Lake Louise train station, there are also tables in vintage railroad dining cars. The food,

mostly West Coast, includes herb-crusted salmon, burgers, Caesar salad, steaks and buffalo. There's a lounge bar and in good weather you can enjoy a barbecue in the station garden.
✉ 200 Sentinel Road ☎ 403/522-2600; www.lakelouisestation.com
🕑 Daily 11:30am–midnight

💎💎💎💎 Post Hotel ($$$)
One of the best restaurants in the Rockies serving a sophisticated fusion of European, Canadian, California and Asian cooking – Albertan beef, foie gras and fresh scallops are just a hint of the culinary delights, all underpinned by a selection of over 2,000 wines. There's an "elegant casual" dress code.
✉ 200 Pipestone Road ☎ 403/522-3989; www.posthotel.com
🕑 Daily 5–10pm

VANCOUVER, BRITISH COLUMBIA

💎💎💎 Aurora Bistro ($$$)
A strong West Coast ethos distinguishes this multi award-winning restaurant where ingredients are locally sourced and organic. Dishes such as halibut cheek schnitzel show the culinary flair, and the wine list is proudly British Columbian.
✉ 24520 Main Street ☎ 604/873-9944 🕑 Dinner from 5:30pm daily; brunch Sat–Sun 10–2

💎💎💎 C ($$$)
Vancouver's best fish and seafood restaurant has a waterside setting with great views. The food is intense and imaginative, with a heavy Asian influence – Arctic char or sea bass, for example, served with a rich wrap or noodles.
✉ 2 - 600 Howe Street ☎ 604/681-1164 🕑 Lunch Mon–Fri, dinner daily

💎💎 Cardero's Restaurant ($$)
An enviable location on the West End waterfront enhances the experience at this busy restaurant where the seafood emphasis translates into delicious dishes. Inside is marine cosiness, and the outer decking offers views of seriously expensive cruisers.
✉ 1583 Coal Harbour Quay ☎ 604/669-7666 🕑 Lunch and dinner

CinCin ($$)
The food – rotisserie meat, fish and game – is predominantly Italian, but you can also eat paella and a wide variety of other dishes. The bar is open between meals for antipasti (appetizers) and pizza from the wood-fired oven. The pastries, bread and ice cream are all homemade.
1154 Robson Street, near Bute Street 604/688-7338 Lunch Mon–Fri, dinner daily

Le Crocodile ($$$)
Le Crocodile serves hearty French bistro dishes – steak tartare, beef tenderloin, rabbit, foie gras and rich desserts. It's a good place for a treat, and not too far from downtown.
100-909 Burrard Street (entrance on Smithe Street) 604/669-4298 Lunch Mon–Fri, dinner Mon–Sat

YOHO NATIONAL PARK, BRITISH COLUMBIA
Truffle Pig's Café ($–$$)
This popular place is part of the Kicking Horse Lodge in the tiny village of Field and is known for its local and regional sourcing and organic preferences. General supplies are also available.
TransCanada Highway, Field 250/343-6462 Breakfast, lunch and dinner daily

SHOPPING
ARTS AND CRAFTS
Crafthouse
Non-profit gallery/shop of the Crafts Association of British Columbia, with an imaginative range of ceramics, fabrics, furniture and glass, along with metal and wood objects.
1386 Cartwright Street, Granville Island, Vancouver, British Columbia 604/687-7270; www.cabc.net Daily 10:30–5:30. Closed Mon in Jan

CLOTHES AND ACCESSORIES
Brick Shirt House
See page 70.

FIRST NATIONS ART

Banff Indian Trading Post

Superb selection of First Nations goods – arts, crafts etc.

✉ 101 Cave Avenue, corner of Birch Avenue, Banff, Alberta ☎ 403/762-2456

Dorothy Grant

See page 70.

Inuit Gallery of Vancouver

See page 70.

MALLS AND DEPARTMENT STORES

The Landing

A classy mall, built around a restored 1915 heritage warehouse in Gastown.

✉ 375 Water Street, Vancouver, British Columbia ☎ 604/453-5050

Metropolis at Metrotown

See page 70.

MARKET

Granville Island Public Market

See page 71.

SPECIALTY STORES

Approach at the Station

See page 71.

Murchie's Tea & Coffee

Murchie's has been selling fine tea and coffee since 1894 and embraces the Fair Trade ethic. You can also buy coffeemakers and teapots and get afternoon tea ($$).

✉ 825 West Pender Street, Vancouver, British Columbia ☎ 604/669-0783

🕒 Mon–Fri 8:30–6, Sat 9:30–6, Sun 12–5

Totem Ski Shop

See page 71.

ENTERTAINMENT AND NIGHTLIFE

BANFF, ALBERTA

The Banff Centre

Arts, culture and conference venue with varied events.

✉ 107 Tunnel Mountain Drive (on slope of Tunnel Mountain) ☎ 403/762-6100 (or 6301 for box office); www.banffcentre.ca 🕓 Year-round

JASPER, ALBERTA

Atha-B Club

The liveliest DJ dancing in town, plus live music most nights.

✉ Athabasca Hotel, 510 Patricia Street ☎ 780/852-3386, 877/542-8422 (toll-free) 🕓 Daily 4pm–2am

VANCOUVER, BRITISH COLUMBIA

Bar None

International and local DJs play disco, R&B, hip hop, soul and the latest sounds.

✉ 1222 Hamilton Street ☎ 604/689-7000

The Cellar

An intimate jazz club hosting some of the best performers.

✉ 3611 West Broadway Street ☎ 604/738-1959

Queen Elizabeth Theatre Complex

Consists of the Vancouver Playhouse and the Queen Elizabeth Theatre, home of the Vancouver Opera and Ballet.

✉ 600 Hamilton Street ☎ 604/665-3050 (no box office – contact Ticketmaster) 🕓 Year-round

Republic

Has an up-top dance floor, and a lower level lounge for chilling.

✉ 958 Granville Street ☎ 604/669-3266

WHISTLER, BRITISH COLUMBIA

Rainbow Theatre

The oldest movie theater in Whistler. Hosts the film festival (➤ 25).

✉ 4010 Whistler Way ☎ 604/932-2422

The Pacific Coast

The most westerly part of Western Canada lies beside the spectacularly beautiful but wild Pacific Ocean – there's little "pacific" about it here! Deeply indented by fjords and surrounded by towering peaks, the coast is rugged, with a multitude of islands offshore. The largest and best known is Vancouver Island in the south. In the north lies the Queen Charlotte archipelago, mist-shrouded home of the First Nation Haida people.

Between them, the islands protect the Inside Passage waterway and, penetrating deep inland, the river valleys of the Skeena and the Bella Coola offer dramatic scenery. The Pacific Coast also offers the stately capital of British Columbia, Victoria. Set on a beautiful harbor, with views across the Strait of Juan de Fuca to the mountains of Washington State, U.S.A., it is a charming, fascinating and very accessible city.

Victoria

VICTORIA

Victoria, capital of British Columbia, sits on the southernmost tip of Vancouver Island, and has one of the finest natural harbors in the world. This former Hudson's Bay Company trading post (1843) prospered in the 1860s as prospectors stopped off en route to the Chilcotin gold fields. It was named in honor of Queen Victoria, and the city has maintained its strong links with Britain, while forging a unique identity of its own.

Today this small, sedate city with its quaint English air, leafy old town, delightful old-fashioned shopping streets and exquisite harbor is a world away from the hustle and bustle of most provincial capitals. It's an easy place to explore on foot – most of what you will want to see is concentrated on or around the Inner Harbour and the Old Town. Foremost among Victoria's attractions are the Royal British Columbia Museum (➤ 119), one of Canada's finest, and the fascinating Maritime Museum (➤ 117).

Craigdarroch Castle, on the outskirts at Rockland, is the Victorian Gothic home of coal magnate Robert Dunsmuir, who moved to Canada from Scotland in 1851. It has some of the finest stained and leaded glass in western Canada and many flamboyant architectural features. Whale-watching trips from the harbor are among the most popular activites, with opportunities for spotting orcas (killer whales), grays and humpbacks, harbor and Dall's porpoises, harbor and elephant seals, and sea lions.

14L

Victoria Visitor Information Centre 812 Wharf Street 250/953-2033, 800/663-3883; www.tourismvictoira.com Jun–Aug daily 8:30–8:30; Sep–May daily 9–5

Craigdarroch Castle

1050 Joan Crescent 250/592-5323; www.craigdarrochcastle.com

Mid-Jun to early Sep daily 9–7; early Sep to mid-Jun daily 10–4:30

Moderate

Downtown Victoria

North of the Inner Harbour (► 116) is the downtown area, a delightful mix of historic buildings, stores, restaurants and pubs. It has a "village" atmosphere and is very walkable. Victoria is one of the liveliest cities in Canada for entertainment all year round. Check the visitor center for the program of events and activities.

Victoria's Chinatown, the third largest in Canada, centers on Fisgard Street and tiny Fan Tan Alley, named after a Chinese card game. The two stone chimeras (mythical beasts) by the Gate of Harmonious Interest were a gift from Suzhou in China. It is said they will come to life when an honest politican walks between them.

There's little to the north worth exploring, so head south on Government Street or Wharf Street (► 121, walk) toward the Inner Harbour. The side streets east and west of Government Street are full of interesting shops, restaurants and bars.

Cafés in Bastion Square and Government Street ($–$$)

Inner Harbour

The lively Inner Harbour is the atmospheric heart of Victoria, a sweeping waterfront fringing the city's downtown (➤ 115). A stroll around its promenade is a great way to take in several of the city's best-known attractions. The upper promenade wall along the inner harbor features a series of fascinating plaques known as the "Parade of Ships," detailing famous vessels and maritime events. A handsome statue of the great seaman James Cook holds center stage. Highly entertaining buskers perform nightly on the lower promenade. It's also fun to take a ride on one of the tiny ferries that buzz around the harbor. Opposite the Infocentre on Wharf Street is the monumental Fairmont Empress Hotel. Other attractions on the harbor include sightseeing cruises and whale-watching trips.

Tea at the Fairmont Empress Hotel (➤ 130)

Maritime Museum

The Maritime Museum, a cut above most museums of its kind, is home to an exquisite collection of artifacts that explore British Columbia's seafaring history. Housed in the historic 1889 Provincial Law Courts on Bastion Square, its galleries cover everything marine, including exploration, piracy, whaling and fishing, shipbuilding, classic boats and BC ferries. There's fascinating maritime memorabilia such as model ships, uniforms, old photographs and ships' bells. Two rare globes that were created after Captain Cook returned to England with new mapping information are among the prize possessions. The galleries themselves are superbly decorated with beautiful woodwork, including walnut, cedar and oak, and this makes a particularly attractive setting for the exhibitions.

✉ 28 Bastion Square ☎ 250/385-4222, ext 103; www.mmbc.bc.ca 🕓 Mid-Jun to mid-Sep daily 9:30–5; mid-Sep to mid-Jun daily 9:30–4:30 💲 Moderate

Parliament Buildings

The beautiful, domed 1893 Parliament Buildings, the seat of BC's Legislative Assembly, overlook the Inner Harbour and are worthy of a visit for their modern Gothic Revival-style architecture (by prolific architect Francis Rattenbury), a stately reminder of British colonial influence. You can take a free guided tour inside, and when the Legislature is in session you can sit in the public gallery and watch, but the main attraction is the ornate exterior detail. A gilded statue of George Vancouver, the first European to sail around Vancouver Island, tops the central dome, while a rather flattering statue of a tall, slim and elegant Queen Victoria, symbol of the city's historic infatuation with all things British, overlooks the formal gardens at the front. At night the entire building is illuminated by thousands of tiny lights.

www.legis.gov.bc.ca

501 Belleville Street 250/387-3046, 800/663-7867 (toll-free) Daily 8:30–5. Closed weekends Oct–Apr Free

Royal British Columbia Museum

The superlative RBCM is regarded as one of the top ten museums in North America and really deserves two days to do it justice. Its three galleries showcase the natural history of the region, provincial history and the Pacific Northwest's First Nations with excellent displays and some dramatic dioramas.

The Natural History Gallery is divided into two separate sections: Living Land, Living Sea opens in dramatic style with a life-size woolly mammoth and goes on to deal with climate change, while the state-of-the-art Open Ocean, with its dark tunnels, takes you on a gripping submarine tour of the sea and deep ocean.

The Modern History Gallery explores British Columbia's history after the arrival of European settlers. Its most impressive exhibit is the recreation of a turn-of-the-20th-century street, complete with cobblestones and rumbling train sounds.

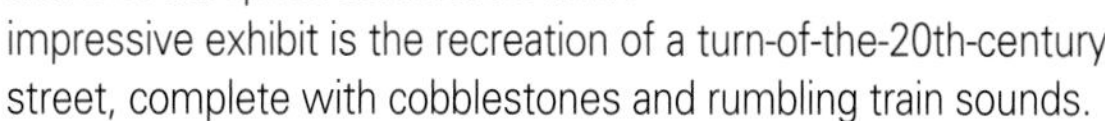

The centerpiece of the First Nations Gallery is the reconstructed, full-size ceremonial longhouse of Chief Kwakwabalasami, with an excellent audiovisual display. Every August the museum holds a three-day outdoor festival celebrating BC's First Nations.

www.royalbcmuseum.bc.ca

675 Belleville Street 250/356-7226, 888/447-7977 (toll-free in North America) Museum: daily 9–5 (Fri–Sat until 10pm); IMAX: daily 10–8 Expensive Café ($)

a walk around downtown Victoria

This walk takes you through the heart of old Victoria, touching on the harbor area, Market Square and Chinatown.

From the Infocentre head north on Government Street, ducking into the smaller streets that run across it from east to west. The first is Courtney Street, followed by Broughton then Fort. Turn right down Broughton Street.

Drop into the Wine Barrel at No. 644, just after Broad Street, for top British Columbian and other vintages.

Go back and turn onto Broad Street, past Pagliacci's restaurant, then turn left on Fore Street to return to Government Street.

Note the building, No.1022, on the opposite west corner of Government Street with Lower Fort Street. Various plaques and pavement inscriptions denote the former heart of Fort Victoria, built in 1843 by the Hudson's Bay Company

Turn right (north) along Government Street and pass View Street on your right. Turn right into Trounce Alley.

Trounce Alley is an attractive narrow street filled with specialty stores and boutiques.

Turn left at Broad Street, cross Yates Street then turn left at the top of Broad Street on Johnson Street. Cross Government Street and a short way down the westerly continuation of Johnson Street on the right is an entrance to Market Square.

Explore Market Square, then return to Johnson Street and turn right.

At the bottom of Johnson Street turn right along Store Street. Take the second right (Fisgard Street, unmarked).

This is the heart of Victoria's Chinatown. Halfway down the street on the right is the narrow Fan Tan Alley (➤ 115).

Return to Store Street and turn left. At Johnson Street, keep ahead onto the continuation, Wharf Street. After about 175m (190yds) detour left into Bastion Square, location of the Maritime Museum (➤ 117). Return to Wharf Street and turn left for the Inner Harbour.

Distance 2.4km (1.5 miles)
Time 1.5 hours. Allow extra time for window-shopping, refreshment stops and visiting museums
Start/end point Inner Harbour Infocentre
Lunch Pagliacci's (➤ 132)

More to see on the Pacific Coast

BUTCHART GARDENS

Best places to see, ➤ 38–39.

CATHEDRAL GROVE

Although this 136ha (336-acre) park is officially called MacMillan Provincial Park, most people know it as Cathedral Grove. The Grove is famous for its giant 800-year-old Douglas fir trees, the largest of which has a circumference of 9m (29ft) and stands 76m (249ft) high. Well-marked trails lead through these majestic stands of forest, and following the south loop you really do feel as if you are within a mighty cathedral, formed by the high canopy of elegant, moss-draped trees. For many years, forest areas adjoining Cathedral Grove have been the center of controversy over logging activities.

North of the highway a trail leads to Cameron Lake, where you can swim or have a picnic, or hike in neighboring Little Qualicum Falls Park, west of Parksville, with impressive waterfalls that cascade down into a rocky gorge in a beautiful forest setting.

✚ 14L ✉ Off Highway 4, 29km (18 miles) west of Parksville, British Columbia
☎ 250/954-4600 🕐 Daily dawn–dusk
✋ Free

CHEMAINUS

The small, former logging town of Chemainus, 80km (50 miles) north of Victoria, is Canada's largest outdoor art gallery. Over 250,000 visitors come each year to view the fascinating collection of murals that adorn the walls and buildings downtown.

The first were commissioned in 1983 to revitalize the town after it began to decline following the closure of its sawmill, the mainstay of the local economy for 120 years. There are now 34 murals, with subjects ranging from a 19th-century brigantine to portraits of First Nations people. The murals are scattered around the town and as you move from one to the next you will learn all about Chemainus's history. In July and August the town celebrates its annual Festival of Murals.

The town itself is a delight, with its pretty painted clapboard houses, antiques shops, boutiques and coffee houses. It is also the departure point for ferry rides to two little islands nearby, Thetis and Kuper.

www.chemainus.com

14L

Visitor InfoCentre 9796 Willow Street, Chemainus, British Columbia 250/246-3944.

NANAIMO

Nanaimo is Vancouver Island's second biggest city, and the attractive waterfront is always busy with freighters, barges and fishing boats. Follow the Harbourside Walkway and stop by the Bastion, an original Hudson's Bay Company fort and now part of the nearby **Nanaimo District Museum,** which celebrates the town's major industry – coal. It also gives an insight into early coastal life on the island and has reproduction castings from Petroglyph Provincial Park. During the last weekend in July, the town hosts the annual Great International World Bathtub Race over the 53km (33 miles) across Georgia Strait to Kitsilano Beach.

www.nanaimo.ca

14L

Tourism Nanaimo 2290 Bowen Road, Nanaimo, British Columbia 250/756-0106, 800/663-7337 (toll-free) Early May–Aug daily 9–6; Sep–early Oct Mon–Fri 9–5, Sat–Sun 10–4; early Oct–early May Mon–Fri 9–5, Sat 10–4

Nanaimo District Museum

100 Museum Way 250/753-1821; www.nanaimomuseum.ca

May–early Sep daily 10–5; early Sep–Apr Tue–Sat 10–5

Inexpensive

PACIFIC RIM NATIONAL PARK

This outstanding park, a combination of mountains, rain forest and wild coastal scenery, is one of the main reasons visitors come to Vancouver Island. It stretches for 128km (80 miles) along the western coast and incorporates the wild and beautiful Broken Islands in Barkley Sound, reached by charter boat (daily Apr–Sep) from Port Alberni. Back on the mainland, Long Beach is a glorious 16km (10-mile) strand of windblown beaches and

crashing waves. Tofino and Ucluelet are the main towns at its northern and southern ends respectively. The popular but challenging 77km (48-mile) West Coast Trail, originally an escape route for shipwrecked sailors to the interior, is not for novices.

14L Moderate Cafés and restaurants at Ucluelet and Tofino ($–$$$)

Pacific Rim Tourism 3100 Kingsway, Port Alberni, British Columbia 250/723-7529, 866/725-7529 (toll-free)

Pacific Rim National Park Office 2185 Ocean Terrace Road, Ucluelet, British Columbia 250/726-3500; www.pc.gc.ca/pacificrim

PRINCE RUPERT AND THE SKEENA VALLEY

Prince Rupert first developed as a Hudson's Bay Company post at the mouth of the Skeena River. Today it is the last ferry stop before Alaska on the Inside Passage (➤ 128–129) from Port Hardy on Vancouver Island, surrounded by vast mountains, deep-cut fjords and a sprinkling of tiny islands. The original 1905 buildings along the waterfront at Cow Bay have been renovated into stores, galleries and restaurants. Leave time to visit the **Museum of Northern British Columbia,** which has an excellent collection of First Nations art and features a traditional longhouse. In summer it runs 2-hour archeology trips to the harbor (phone for details).

The Skeena Valley can be visited as part of the Inside Passage tour (➤ 128–129), by car, VIA Rail or bus from Prince George. Take a detour to New Hazelton to see **'Ksan,** a traditional Gitxsan village, which was created to preserve this rapidly vanishing culture. The site features several tribal longhouses and what is reputedly the world's largest standing totem pole; you will see other fine examples along the way.

14H From Port Hardy, Vancouver Island (15 hours) Air Canada Jazz twice daily from Vancouver (2 hours)

Visitor Centre Suite 100, 215 Cow Bay Road, Prince Rupert, British Columbia 250/624-5637, 800/667-1994 (toll-free)

Museum of Northern British Columbia

100 1st Avenue West 250/624-3207 Jun–Aug Mon–Sat 9–8, Sun 9–5; Sep–May Mon–Sat 9–5 Moderate

'Ksan

New Hazelton, British Columbia 250/842-5544, 877/842-5518 (toll-free) Daily; tours summer only Inexpensive; tours expensive

QUEEN CHARLOTTE ISLANDS (HAIDA GWAII)

These islands lie 128km (80 miles) west of Prince Rupert across the Hecate Strait. Called Haida Gwaii ("islands of the people") by the Haida people, they offer some of the most remote coastal landscape in Canada – snow-topped mountains, sheer-sided fjords, mist-shrouded forests and windswept sandy beaches. This fascinating archipelago consists of the two larger islands of Graham and Moresby and 150 smaller ones.

Graham Island is the most accessible, with a ferry from Prince Rupert to Skidegate. Here the **Haida Gwaii Museum** showcases the traditional Haida culture and history, and geology of the islands. Queen Charlotte City is the administrative center. Sandspit is the only settlement on Moresby Island and starting point for the Gwaii Haanas National Park Reserve, which covers most of the island. Access is only by boat and floatplane, reservations are required and you must attend an orientation session.

13H BC Ferries from Prince Rupert to Skidegate Daily flights from Vancouver and Prince Rupert to Sandspit

Queen Charlotte Visitor Centre 3220 Wharf Street, Queen Charlotte City, British Columbia 250/559-8316; www.qcinfo.ca Summer daily 8–12, 4–9; winter Tue–Sat 12–5

Haida Gwaii Museum

2nd Beach Road, Skidegate, British Columbia 250/559-4643; www.haidagwaii.ca May to mid-Jun Mon–Sat 10–6; mid-Jun to mid-Sep daily 10–6; mid-Sep to Apr Tue–Sat 10–5 Inexpensive

a voyage around the Inside Passage

The Inside Passage is one of the world's most dramatic voyages, offering the chance to see migrating whales and other marine life.

An hour after leaving Port Hardy the boat sails portside (left) of tiny Pine Island, where a lighthouse marks the main entrance to the Inside Passage.

Beyond here is the most exposed section of the journey. The lighthouse on Egg Island has suffered severe damage several times since it was established in 1898. Up ahead the channel narrows and the boat enters FitzHugh Sound.

At its northern end the ship takes a port turn between Hunter and Denny islands, then cruises starboard (right) of Campbell Island, passing McLoughlin Bay, also known as Bella Bella.

Dryad Point marks the northern tip of Campbell Island and the ship feels the full force of the ocean passing through exposed Milbanke Sound before turning to starboard toward Boat Bluff, the halfway point. The next four hours offer the most spectacular experience of the journey as the ship plies the narrowest section – a long sheer-sided fjord stretching off into the distance.

Ten hours from Port Hardy, Butedale comes into view on the port side.

Founded in 1919, Butedale was one of the longest-lived fish cannery villages along the coast, only ceasing production in 1956. Hartley Bay, a traditional Tsimshian

First Nations village, marks the southern tip of Grenville Channel, a 64km (40-mile) long section whose narrowest point is just 500m (1,640ft) wide. Hartley Bay is only accessible by boat or floatplane and is a favorite anchorage for recreational sailors during the summer.

At the northern mouth of the Grenville Channel, on the port side, is the Oona River. From here it's only another two hours to Prince Rupert (► 126–127), passing the bulk shipping terminal on Ridley Island on the starboard side shortly before docking.

Distance 288km (179 miles)
Time 15 hours
Start point Port Hardy, Vancouver Island, British Columbia ✚ 14K
BC Ferries ☎ 250/386-3431, 888/223-3779 (toll-free); www.bcferries.com
End point Prince Rupert, British Columbia ✚ 14H
Refreshments Aboard ship

HOTELS

NANAIMO, BRITISH COLUMBIA

Best Western Dorchester Hotel ($–$$)

A boutique-style hotel with elegant guest rooms overlooking the harbor and city. The service is excellent and the location a plus.

70 Church Street 250/754-6835, 800/661-2449 (toll-free); www.dorchesternanaimo.com

TOFINO, BRITISH COLUMBIA

Wickaninnish Inn ($$$–$$$$)

Spectacularly set on a rocky headland on Vancouver Island's rugged west coast, close to the Pacific Rim National Park, this inn has magnificent ocean and beach views, and private balconies to take full advantage of them.

500 Osprey Lane at Chesterman Beach, PO Box 250, Tofino 250/725-3100, 800/333-4604; www.wickinn.com

VICTORIA, BRITISH COLUMBIA

Abigail's ($$–$$$$)

Located only three blocks from the Inner Harbour and all the attractions of downtown Victoria, this is a lovely small hotel. The rooms are all beautifully furnished with antiques, and some have Jacuzzis and fireplaces. A gourmet breakfast is included in the price, and there's a spa with a variety of treatments.

906 McClure Street 250/388-5363, 866/347-5054; www.abigailshotel.com

Fairmont Empress Hotel ($$–$$$$)

The Empress is an imposing sight in its central position close to the Parliament Building and overlooking the Inner Harbour. Service is excellent, as are the amenities, and all the rooms are well-furnished. Elegant and expensive afternoon teas, in true British style, are served to some 80,000 visitors a year.

721 Government Street 250/384-8111, 866/540-4429 (reservations, toll-free); www.fairmont.com/empress

The Royal Scot ($$–$$$$)

Set in its own attractive grounds, the Royal Scot offers a good selection of rooms and suites in a convenient location for Victoria's Inner Harbour and Downtown.

425 Quebec Street 250/388-5463, 800/663-7515 (toll-free); www.royalscot.com

RESTAURANTS

NANAIMO, BRITISH COLUMBIA

Mahle House ($$)

The menu here changes weekly, but the food always uses the freshest local meat and fish. Pricy, but worthwhile, is the seafood selection of wild sockeye salmon, scallops and prawns dressed with a saffron, garlic and olive oil sauce and lemon oil.

2104 Hemer Road 250/722-3621 Closed lunch and Mon–Tue

PRINCE RUPERT, BRITISH COLUMBIA

Green Apple Halibut and Chips ($)

This shack is an institution, renowned for its fresh halibut and fries.

301 McBride Street 250/627-1666 Daily, times vary at the whim of the owner

QUALICUM BEACH, BRITISH COLUMBIA

Old Dutch Inn ($$)

Servers dressed in Dutch costume add to the experience and there are wonderful sea views. In addition to world-famous pastries, there are Dutch specialties on the menu. Reservations are recommended in summer.

2690 Island Highway 250/752-6914 Breakfast, lunch and dinner daily

TOFINO, BRITISH COLUMBIA

Pointe ($$$)

Jutting out into the ocean, this upscale restaurant has breathtaking views. Canadian West Coast cuisine features fresh seafood.

Wickaninnish Inn, Osprey Lane/Chesterman Beach 250/725-3100 Breakfast, lunch and dinner daily

VICTORIA, BRITISH COLUMBIA

Brasserie l'Ecole ($$)

A modern bistro where the style is good, hearty French food using the best local produce for dishes that won't burn a hole in your pocket.

1715 Government Street 250/475-6260 Tue–Sat 5:30–11pm

Café Brio ($$$)

Tuscan flavor is the signature at this distinctive eatery where a touch of theater has gone into the fittings and decor. The food is exceptional, with main dishes of pan-roasted halibut or duck breast only part of an exciting menu that includes crafted charcuterie.

944 Fort Street 250/383-0009 Daily from 5:30pm

Canoe Brewpub and Restaurant ($$–$$$)

Located in an 1890s building, this popular pub and restaurant offers award-winning beers and a terrific selection of main dishes and bar meals. Live music Wednesday and Thursday nights.

450 Swift Street 250/361-1940 11:30am until late

Haultain Fish and Chips ($$)

This is one of the best fish and chip shops in Victoria; the fish is always wonderfully fresh, and there's a take-out service.

1127 Haultain 250/383-8332 Tue–Sat 11:30–8, Sun 3:30–7:30

Pagliacci's ($–$$)

Reservations aren't taken here and it's very popular, so arrive early. The food – a mixture of Italian, Jewish, West Coast and Brooklyn – includes homemade pasta, chicken and veal, with the restaurant's famous cheesecake on the dessert menu. Live music most nights.

1011 Broad Street 250/386-1662 Mon–Thu 11:30–10, Fri–Sat 11:30–11, Sun 10–10

Re-Bar ($–$$)

Bright, quirky decor complements the cheerful bohemian style at this popular vegetarian restaurant noted for its fresh fruit and veggie juices and well-sourced produce.

50 Bastion Square 250/361-9223 Mon–Wed 8:30am–9pm, Thu–Sat 8:30am–10pm, Sun 8:30–3:30

Red Fish Blue Fish ($–$$)
See page 59.

SHOPPING

ARTS AND CRAFTS

Artevo
Victoria venue for world collections of paintings, ceramics, glass work, sculpture and jewelry by numerous fine artists.
616 Fort Street, Victoria, British Columbia 250/389-1699, 888/389-1699 (toll-free)

Cowichan Trading Co. Ltd.
First Nations crafts and a wide range of souvenirs, including jewelry, moccasins, traditional Cowichan knitwear and pewter.
1328 Government Street, Victoria, British Columbia 250/383-0321

Royal British Columbia Museum Shop
First Nations artwork including gold and silver jewelry, ceremonial sticks, totem poles and masks.
675 Belleville Street, Victoria, British Columbia 250/356-0505

CLOTHING

Jan Donaldson Designs
The home and studio of the fiber artist and clothing designer who hosted her own TV crafts show when she lived in Montréal.
3039 Lashman Avenue, Chemainus, British Columbia 250/748-8841, 800/442-6446 (toll-free) By appointment

FOOD AND DRINK

Roger's Chocolates
The place to shop for hand-crafted, preservative-free chocolates.
913 Government Street, Victoria, British Columbia 250/881-8771 Daily 9–9

MALLS AND DEPARTMENT STORES

The Bay

Victoria's key department store, with a huge selection of goods.

✉ The Bay Centre, 1150 Douglas Street, Victoria, British Columbia ☎ 250/952-5680 🕐 Mon–Wed 9:30–6, Thu–Fri 9:30–9, Sat 9:30–6, Sun 11–6

MARKET

Salt Spring Island Saturday Market

This Gulf island is renowned for its artist/artisan community and for its organic market gardens. Their output is on sale here.

✉ Centennial Park, Ganges, British Columbia ☎ 250/537-4448 🕐 Late Mar–late Oct Sat 8:30–3:30

ENTERTAINMENT AND NIGHTLIFE

VICTORIA, BRITISH COLUMBIA

Belfry

This old church is now a theater, producing high-quality shows; also hosts pop and jazz concerts.

✉ 1291 Gladstone Avenue ☎ 250/385-6815; www.belfry.bc.ca 🕐 Aug to mid-May

Irish Times

A lively mock trad pub that offers decent food with live music that has echoes of Irish foot-stomping bars.

✉ 1200 Government Street ☎ 250/383-7775 🕐 Daily 11am–1am

Royal and McPherson

The Victoria Symphony and the Pacific Opera Victoria are based in this superb early 20th-century building.

✉ 805 Broughton Street ☎ 250/386-6121, 888/717-6121; www.rmts.bc.ca 🕐 Year-round

The Prairies

Canada's Prairie provinces – Manitoba, Saskatchewan and Alberta from east to west – are not just the flat grasslands that famously stretch to the horizon. They actually rise in stages, from sea level around Hudson Bay, through the Manitoba Escarpment and the Missouri Coteau, to a height of more than 1,200m (3,937ft) near the foothills of the Rocky Mountains. The region incorporates a variety of landscapes – the frozen wastes of the northern tundra, the canyons and dramatic moonscapes of the Alberta Badlands, the uplands of the Cypress Hills and, of course, those huge wheat fields and cattle ranges.

You get an overall view of the enormity of the Prairies from a plane, but take the VIA Rail train from Toronto to Edmonton or drive the Yellowhead Highway or TransCanada for a more immediate experience. Vast Prairie skies, stunning sunsets and the shimmering colors of the aurora borealis (Northern Lights) are a major complement to this wide, open land – a region that drew a diverse cultural mix of immigrants from across Europe.

WINNIPEG

Winnipeg, increasingly known as the "Heart of the Continent," is fast emerging as a vibrantly independent city with a cultural and culinary scene to rival other major Canadian urban centers. Hot spots include Corydon Avenue with its lively shopping, restaurant and café culture, Downtown and the Exchange District, while the superb Forks area is packed with modern restaurants, bars, shops and attractions. Across the Red River is the "French Quarter" of St. Boniface. One of Winnipeg's finest assets is the delightful Assiniboine Park, alongside the Assiniboine River, where you will find Winnipeg Zoo, the English Garden and the Leo Mol Sculpture Garden. In the churchyard of St. Boniface Basilica is the grave of Louis Riel (1844–85), leader of the Métis – a mixed-race, French-speaking nation – and a famous participant in the Northwest Rebellion.

www.destinationwinnipeg.ca

24M

Tourism Winnipeg 259 Portage Avenue, Winnipeg, Manitoba 204/943-1970, 800/665-0204 (toll-free)

Centennial Centre

This modern complex was built as part of Canada's centennial celebrations in 1967 and is home to the outstanding Manitoba Museum (► 46–47). It also houses Oseredok (184 Alexander Avenue E), the Ukrainian cultural and educational center.

The focus of its lively performing arts center is the Centennial Concert Hall, home of Winnipeg's Royal Ballet (the oldest dance company in Canada), its Opera company and the Winnipeg Symphony Orchestra, in addition to hosting traveling international classical and modern performances.

Centennial Concert Hall

555 Main Street 204/956-1360, 204/780-3333 (Ticketmaster); www.mbccc.ca Depends on performance Depends on performance

Downtown

Downtown Winnipeg stretches north and west of the junction of the Red and Assiniboine rivers, and includes the busy intersection of Portage Avenue and Main Road. Winnipeg Square, a big underground shopping mall, is the heart of the shopping district, with the Winnipeg Art Gallery (➤ 141) and Winnipeg Commodity Exchange (the only agricultural exchange in Canada) nearby. South of the Art Gallery, beyond the Memorial Park, is the splendid neoclassical Legislative Building. The Golden Boy statue on top of the 74m-high (243ft) dome of the "Ledge" is one of the best-known symbols of Manitoba. East along Broadway from the "Ledge" is the **Dalnavert National Historic Museum,** a Queen Anne Revival-style house from the 1890s with handsome furnishings and stained-glass windows.

259 Portage Avenue 204/943-1970; www.destinationwinnipeg.ca

Dalnavert National Historic Museum

61 Carlton Street 204/943-2835; www.mhs.mb.ca Wed–Sat 11–6, Sun 12–4. Closed Mon–Tue

Inexpensive

The Exchange District and Market Square

The regenerated Exchange District, a National Historic Site, is a lively area of bars, restaurants and nightlife in the city's 19th-century heart. Once a run-down area of warehouses and railroad yards, it has a wealth of fine early 20th-century architecture. This includes the 1912 Confederation Life building, an early skyscraper; the lavish 1913 Pantages Theatre; the 1903 British Bank of North America; and the 1903 Criterion Hotel, with its rare terra cotta facade.

Between June and early September walking tours of the Exchange District and Market Square, lasting between one and two hours, depart (10am and 2pm daily; moderate) from the information center on Old Market Square, a place that becomes a focus for outdoor performances of every kind during the summer.

www.exchangedistrict.org

Information Office 133 Albert Street, Old Market Square 204/942-6716

The Forks National Historic Site

Located in the center of Winnipeg, where the Red and Assiniboine rivers meet, is the Forks, originally a meeting place for the First Nations. Today this revitalized district is a lively and colorful gathering place for locals and visitors alike, who come to enjoy its historic landmarks, leafy parks, river walkways and excellent marketplace. Here, former Canadian Pacific Railway buildings have been transformed into a shopping, eating and entertainment complex with interpretive displays, sculptures and a wide range of events for all the family. The riverside walk is a great way to spend a summer's evening, and there are many open-air events, plus several "Buskstops" for street entertainment.

www.theforks.com

25 Forks Market Road 204/983-6757 Free Restaurants and cafés ($–$$$)

Manitoba Children's Museum

Located at the Forks Historical Site, next to the Johnson Terminal, this terrific museum is an exciting hands-on learning center for children, devoted to fun and make-believe. In the Wonderworks Gallery they can design a city, play with water and make electrical connections. In the Prehistoric Playground they can interact with baby dinosaurs and make a juvenile *T-Rex* come to life. There's a TV studio where they can create and present their own shows, or operate the cameras. It's a family-oriented attraction and the eclectic mixture of historical, scientific and natural displays appeals to children and adults alike.

www.childrensmuseum.com

45 Forks Market Road 204/924-4000 Daily 9:30–4:30 (also 4:30–8, Fri–Sat) Inexpensive Café ($–$$)

Manitoba Museum
Best places to see, ➤ 46–47.

Winnipeg Art Gallery

Winnipeg Art Gallery is one of the city's architectural showpieces. Built in local Tyndall stone, it resembles a ship rising out of the water. It includes over 22,500 works, and contains one of the world's largest collections of contemporary Inuit art, with more than 10,000 carvings, prints, drawings and textiles. The gallery also features changing exhibitions by Manitoban, Canadian and international artists, past and present. A highlight is the Gort Collection of Gothic and Northern Renaissance altar paintings and tapestries from the 16th century. An added bonus is the wonderful rooftop restaurant, with panoramic views over the city.

www.wag.mb.ca

✉ 300 Memorial Boulevard ☎ 204/786-6641, 204/789-1760 (information)
🕐 Tue–Sun 11–5 (also 5–9 Thu) Moderate Brio Restaurant ($$)

a walk around downtown Winnipeg

This route connects many of Winnipeg's most frequently visited attractions.

Start at The Forks (➤ 140). Walk along the riverside toward the Esplanade Riel and Provencher Bridge and cross the Red River by the futuristic pedestrian bridge. Turn right on Tache Avenue and walk one block to the heart of Winnipeg's French Quarter.

Stroll among the ruins of St. Boniface Cathedral and its graveyard, containing the tomb of Louis Riel (➤ 136).

Recross the river and take the first right, Pioneer

Avenue. You'll pass the CanWest Global Park baseball field on your left and walk underneath the railroad bridge before entering the Exchange District (► 139). Go left along any of the cross streets – Lombard, McDermot or Bannatyne – to reach Main Street.

Turn right for the Manitoba Museum (► 46–47).

Cross Main Street with care, turn left and then right onto Portage Avenue, the city's main shopping street. Continue past Portage Place Shopping Centre (six blocks along on the right) to The Bay department store on the left. Turn left here along Memorial Boulevard.

On the opposite side of the road from The Bay is the Winnipeg Art Gallery (► 141).

Follow Memorial Boulevard alongside Memorial Park to the Legislative Building (► 138). Cross Broadway, with care, then turn left.

Soon you pass the monumental Hotel Fort Garry, famed for its ornate bar. Turn right down Fort Street. In about 50m (55yds) turn left through the scant but evocative remains of Upper Fort Garry. There are proposals to renovate the site.

Continue through the Fort to Main Street. Turn left and cross at lights to the magnificent Rail Union Station. Turn right in front of the station and then in 50m (55yds) turn left beneath a rail underpass into The Forks.

Distance 7km (4.3 miles)
Time 4 hours (excluding exploring the attractions)
Start/end point The Forks
Lunch The Forks, Exchange District, Manitoba Museum, or Portage Place Shopping Centre ($–$$$)

CALGARY

From its beginnings as a North West Mounted Police fort in 1875, Calgary has prospered, first on the back of agriculture, and since the 1970s from the area's burgeoning oil and gas industry. This wealth has helped pay for the city's shiny high-rise center, with its mirrored skyscrapers, glamorous corporate buildings and urban expressways.

Set in the rolling foothills of the Alberta Rockies, Calgary enjoys a backdrop of gorgeous scenery and is perfectly placed for exploring the mountains to the west, but the city itself deserves a visit too. The terrific Glenbow Museum alone would make it worthwhile, but there is also one of the biggest zoos in Canada, a lively heritage park and a leafy urban park set on an island in the middle of the Bow River.

The Calgary Stampede is the city's best-known attraction, 10 days of parades and rodeos that draw over a million visitors a year from around the world (➤ 25).

www.tourismcalgary.com

18L

Tourism Calgary, 101-9 Avenue SW ☎ 403/750-2362

Calgary Tower

The 1968 Calgary Tower, in the heart of downtown, is one of the city's most distinctive landmarks. At 193m (633ft), it was once the city's tallest structure, though these days it has been superceded by three others. High-speed elevators take visitors to the top for a great all-round view of the city and its setting. On a clear day you can see as far as the peaks of the Rockies to the west and the rippling prairies stretching away to the east. You can also look directly downward on the glass floor, installed in 2005. The tower lies across the street from the Glenbow Museum (➤ 148–149), close to the main shopping malls.

www.calgarytower.com

✉ 101 9th Avenue SW

☎ 403/266-7171

🕓 Jun–early Sep daily 7:30am–10pm; early Sep–May daily 9:30–9:30 ✋ Moderate

🍴 Snack bar and Sky 360 revolving restaurant ($–$$$)

Calgary Zoo

Calgary Zoo covers 32ha (79 acres) to the east of the city and is one of the best zoological gardens in Canada. It has made a great effort to accommodate the animals in habitats that are as near "natural" as possible, including rain forest, savanna and mountain environments, encompassing Africa, Eurasia and Australian sections. There are also underwater viewing areas for watching fish and marine mammals. Live animals, from gorillas to grizzlies, provide an intriguing and educational experience.

The Prehistoric Park is particularly popular with children, with its displays of life-size dinosaur replicas, model volcano and more than 100 species of plants. Here you can discover what life in western Canada might have been like when these mighty creatures reigned supreme in the swamplands of Alberta. The beautiful Botanical Gardens contain over 4,000 plant species and include a tropical rain forest, an arid garden and butterfly gardens.

www.calgaryzoo.org

1300 Zoo Road NE 403/232-9300, 800/588-9993 (toll-free) Daily 9–5 Expensive Cafés and kiosks ($)

Fort Calgary Historic Site

Calgary began life as a wooden stockade built in six weeks by the North West Mounted Police in 1875 to curb the lawlessness of the illicit whiskey trade spilling over the U.S. border. It's long since gone, and what you see today is a reconstruction of the first fort on the original site, set in lovely parkland. You can watch history unfold as the fort and its interpretive center recall the daily lives of the people of Calgary from 1875 to 1940, using a mixture of evocative photographs, dynamic exhibits, written documents and interactive interpretation. The site includes a replica of the 1888 barracks, and close by is Hunt House (not open) and Deane House, built in 1906 by Superintendent Deane, the local head of the Mounties.

www.fortcalgary.ab.ca

750 9th Avenue SE 403/290-1875 Daily 9–5 Moderate

Deane House Restaurant ($–$$); Mess Kitchen ($–$$)

Glenbow Museum

The Glenbow is one of western Canada's finest museums, home to an impressive collection of over a million artifacts, photographs and works of art. Its outstanding art, historical displays and First Nations exhibits provide the perfect introduction to the area, using film, music, sound, dance, sculpture and hands-on displays. The Blackfoot Gallery – Nitsitapiisinni: Our Way of Life, focuses on the history of the Blackfoot people, highlighting their lives, culture, art and their suffering following the arrival of Europeans. On the same floor is Mavericks: An Incorrigible History of Alberta. Other galleries illustrate the history of the Inuit and the mixed-race French-speaking Métis, the Riel Uprising, the fur trade, the North West Mounted Police and the development of the oil and gas industries. Art in Asia is also featured, with a superb collection of sacred Buddhist and Hindu artifacts, and there is a compelling celebration of African achievement, Where Symbols Meet, as well as a glittering collection of gems, stones and minerals.

www.glenbow.org
130 9th Avenue SE 403/268-4100 Museum: daily 9–5 (also 5–9pm Thu). Library: Tue–Fri 10–5 Moderate Manny's Café ($) in foyer of 9th Avenue entrance

Heritage Park Historical Village

Canada's largest living historic village recreates the sights and sounds of life in Calgary at the turn of the 20th century. Set in 27ha (67 acres) of lush parkland in the heart of Calgary, the village features more than 150 buildings and exhibits with costumed guides in attendance. You can visit the SS *Moyie* sternwheeler and cruise the reservoir, board an authentic steam locomotive, ride around town in a horse-drawn carriage, enjoy the thrills of an antique midway (funfair) or take a stroll down Main Street (circa 1910), lined with stores and saloons. Your entrance fee also entitles you to a free western-style breakfast between 9 and 10am throughout the summer.
www.heritagepark.ca
1900 Heritage Drive SW 403/268-8500 Late May–early Sep daily 9–5; early Sep–early Oct Sat–Sun 9–5 Expensive Choice in park ($–$$)

Prince's Island Park

Peaceful Prince's Island Park, set on an artificial island in the middle of the Bow River, offers a welcome respite from sightseeing, just minutes from downtown Calgary. Accessed by several bridges, this urban oasis of green and shady nooks is free from traffic and is a favorite haven for locals and visitors. The formal gardens and lawns are particularly pleasant in spring and summer and are perfect for a stroll or a picnic (tables are provided) and the outdoor stage is the venue for many musical and cultural events and festivals. One of Calgary's finest restaurants, the River Café (➤ 167), is located on the island.
In the Bow River River Café (➤ 167)

More to see in the Prairies

BATOCHE NATIONAL HISTORIC SITE

It was at Batoche that the Métis, of mixed French and First Nations blood, settled in the 19th century after leaving Red River in Manitoba, but their hope to pursue their traditional way of life in peace was not to be realized. Louis Riel, their charismatic leader, selected the site, strategically overlooking the South Saskatchewan River, as his headquarters and it became the last battlefield in the 1885 rebellion over land titles.

Several original buildings have been restored at the Batoche National Historic Site, including the church, the rectory and the cemetery, which contains the graves of the guerilla leader Gabriel Dumont, who commanded the last stand, Batoche founder Xavier Letendre and the Métis who were killed in the final assault. The displays and audiovisual presentations at the visitor center are excellent, and the helpful costumed staff is on hand to explain more.

21K Wakaw, Saskatchewan 306/423-6227; www.pc.gc.ca/batoche Early May–Sep daily 9–5 Moderate Snack concessions ($)

CARDSTON

The little town of Cardston lies in the foothills of the Rocky Mountains, just a half hour from Waterton Lakes

National Park (➤ 100). It is famous for having the largest Mormon tabernacle outside the U.S. (visitor center and grounds only open), and for its fine carriage museum, one of the largest in North America. Located in 8ha (20 acres) of parkland in the beautiful Lee Creek Valley, the **Remington-Alberta Carriage Centre** has a superb collection of some 250 horse-drawn vehicles. These range from simple buggies and utility wagons to elegant carriages used by royalty and the stagecoaches of the Old West. You can tour the tack room, workshop, stables and corrals, watch skilled craftworkers restore the carriages and meet the horses that pull them.

www.town.cardston.ab.ca

18M

Remington-Alberta Carriage Centre

623 Main Street, Cardston, Alberta 403/653-5139; www.remingtoncentre.com Mid-May to mid-Sep daily 9–6; mid-Sep to mid-May 10–5 Moderate Cafés in town ($)

CHURCHILL

Remote Churchill stands on the southwestern shore of Hudson Bay, at the mouth of the Churchill River, and for several months of the year is an ice-free port, but it is best known as the "Polar Bear Capital of the World." Late autumn is the best time to see the magnificent creatures, just before the bay refreezes. It's also a great place to see abundant bird life, whales, caribou and seals, and tours are available by helicopter, boat or "tundra buggy." Churchill is also a prime spot for observing the Northern Lights.

The **Eskimo Museum** has a vast range of tools, artifacts and carvings that focus on the lifestyle and history of the Inuit. **Fort Prince of Wales,** across the estuary from Churchill, was built by the Hudson's Bay Company between 1731 and 1771, and you can visit its bulwarks, barracks and commander's quarters on a guided boat tour (daily, Jul–Aug). Remember to bring insect repellent – the air teems with insects, especially mosquitoes.

Churchill is not accessible by road – there are scheduled flights and a rail service from Winnipeg, and the two-day journey across the tundra is one of Canada's more fascinating train rides. From late June to early August the ground is a glorious carpet of miniature flowers, including several species of cold-tolerant orchids.

24G

Parks Canada Visitor Reception Centre Bayport Plaza, Churchill, Manitoba 204/675-8863 Choice in town ($–$$$)

Eskimo Museum

La Verendrye Avenue 204/675-2030 Jun–early Nov Tue–Sat 9–12, 1–5; late Nov–May Mon–Sat 1–4:30 Donation

Fort Prince of Wales

204/675-8863 Phone for details

CYPRESS HILLS AND FORT WALSH

The Blackfoot called the Cypress Hills area Ketewius Netumoo – "the hills that shouldn't be." They straddle the border between

Alberta and Saskatchewan, and are the highest point between the Rocky Mountains and Labrador, on the east coast.

Cypress Hills Inter-Provincial Park, the first of its kind in Canada, is a haven of peaceful lodgepole pine forests and rare wild flowers, high forested hills, panoramic views and quiet valleys, and is also home to many native animals such as wapiti (elk), deer, moose and trumpeter swans.

Fort Walsh National Historic Site, accessible from Cypress Hills or Maple Creek (on Highway 271), was a major North West Mounted Police post in the 1880s, and after the force became the Royal Canadian Mounted Police in 1920 it was their horse-breeding center. It has now been reconstructed, with interpretive displays covering the fort's history, the culture of the local First Nations people and background on the North West Mounted Police. Farwell's Trading Post takes you back to the wild days of the illegal whiskey trade in Canada.

Cypress Hills

19M 27km (17 miles) south of Maple Creek, Saskatchewan
306/662-5411 (Saskatchewan); 403/893-3777 (Alberta); www.cypresshills.com Day pass: moderate

Fort Walsh

19M Box 278, Maple Creek, Saskatchewan 306/662-2645; www.pc.gc.ca/walsh Mid-May to early Sep daily 9:30–5:30 Moderate

a drive through Cypress Hills Inter-Provincial Park

Leave Elkwater along the lakeside past the Visitor Information Centre and take the road signposted Ferguson Hill. At the next crossroads go right to Horseshoe Canyon. Head back to the intersection and go straight ahead, then across Route 41 (signposted Elkwater left and the U.S. border right). Follow signs for Reesor Lake.

Much of the 18km (11 miles) to Reesor Lake is a plateau of thick grassland. Look for signs for Bull Trail, a passing point of wagon trains that once plied a north–south route, and the turnoff left for Spruce Coulee. The overview of Reesor Lake is on the right after 14km (8.5 miles). The road then sweeps on around the main body of the lake.

At the western lake head the asphalt gives way to dirt road. Turn left, signposted Fort Walsh.

Fort Walsh is right at an intersection. Immediately to the right after the junction is a monument to Constable Graburn of the North West Mounted Police, the first officer to be killed in the line of duty (on November 12, 1879).

Make another left at the next intersection and after 1.6km (1 mile) enter Saskatchewan. Cross the bridge at Battle Creek. There's a ranger station on the right halfway up the hill. About 14km (8.5 miles) after the border, go right on a paved road; it's 4km (2.5 miles) to Fort Walsh.

Fort Walsh (► 153), just off the main route, offers a wonderful insight into Canadian history.

Return to the main route and turn right in the direction of Maple Creek. At the next T-junction, turn left; watch for a turning to the right, signed GAP Road, (a green sign states "Cypress Hills Road") approaching the other way. The GAP road turnoff is 9km (5.5 miles) from Fort Walsh.

This 22.5km (14-mile) strip of land is a good place to see low-growing wild flowers in spring and summer.

At the end of GAP Road turn right to Loch Leven.

Distance 140km (87 miles)
Time 3 hours
Start point Elkwater ✚ 19M
End point Loch Leven ✚ 19M
Refreshments Elkwater, Loch Leven, Fort Walsh (in season)

Warning: It's not advisable to drive the route after prolonged wet weather as the dirt road section turns into a quagmire.

DINOSAUR PROVINCIAL PARK

Dinosaur Provincial Park was created in 1955 to protect one of the world's most extensive dinosaur fields. Over 300 complete skeletons from 37 different species have been excavated, and new ones are unearthed nearly every year. Scientists now believe that some of the dinosaurs were carried here from farther north by glacial meltwaters and are not actually native to the area.

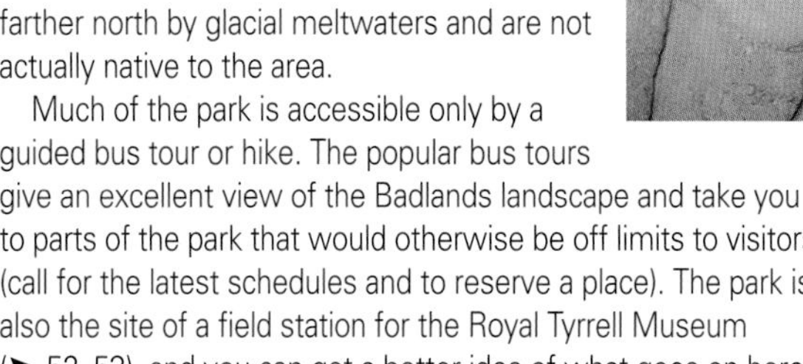

Much of the park is accessible only by a guided bus tour or hike. The popular bus tours give an excellent view of the Badlands landscape and take you to parts of the park that would otherwise be off limits to visitors (call for the latest schedules and to reserve a place). The park is also the site of a field station for the Royal Tyrrell Museum (➤ 52–53), and you can get a better idea of what goes on here by talking to the laboratory technicians who treat the skeletons after they have been excavated.

19L 48km (30 miles) northeast of TransCanada 1 from Brooks, Alberta 403/378-4344; www.cd.gov.ab.ca/parks/dinosaur Daily Free. Bus tours and hikes: moderate Dinosaur Service Centre for snacks ($)

DRUMHELLER AND THE ALBERTA BADLANDS

The little town of Drumheller sits in the valley of the Red Deer River at the heart of the Alberta Badlands. This strange, otherwordly landscape of barren, sunbeaten hills, mud gullies, windblown bluffs and mushroom-shaped hoodoos (rock formations) was created by the action of wind, rain and glacial meltwater during the last Ice Age. The swamplands of Alberta were a haven for dinosaurs and today this region is one of the world's most abundant sources of dinosaur fossils. (Some 96km/60 miles southeast of Drumheller is the Dinosaur Provincial Park, ➤ above.) In Drumheller, the information center is watched

over by the World's Largest Dinosaur, a massive 26m (86ft) high. Visitors can climb the 106 steps inside the beast and gaze out through its open jaws over the town and Badlands beyond.

Drumheller is a good place to pick up the Dinosaur Trail, a 48km (30-mile) circular route linking several historic sights and numerous viewpoints. Major attractions along the way are the Royal Tyrrell Museum (► 52–53) and Horsethief Canyon, with its stunning multilayered walls.

The Hoodoo Trail, 24km (15 miles) southeast of Drumheller on Highway 10, takes you past some bizarre natural rock formations.

18L (Drumheller), 19L (Alberta Badlands)

Drumheller Tourism 60 1st Avenue W, Drumheller, Alberta 866/823-8100 (toll-free in North America); www.canadianbadlands.com; www.traveldrumheller.com Jul–Aug daily 9–9; Sep–Apr daily 10–5:30; May–Jun phone for details

EDMONTON

Edmonton, gateway to the unspoiled north, developed around a Hudson's Bay Company post called Edmonton House. In 1905 it became provincial capital, and the discovery of oil in the region in 1947 gave the city, and Alberta, a huge economic boost.

Downtown is the most attractive part of the city; its ranks of granite and steel skyscrapers fill a tight grid on Jasper Avenue, the main street. At its heart is Churchill Square, dominated by modern buildings. These include City Hall, an interesting building that combines modern architecture with elements from the old City Hall, and the Citadel Theatre, the largest theater complex in Canada. Also here is the **Art Gallery of Alberta,** one of Alberta's oldest cultural institutions, containing over 5,000 historical and contemporary paintings, sculptures, prints, installation works and photographs from Canadian and international artists, with a strong focus on Alberta art.

West of downtown is the massive beaux-arts **Alberta Legislature Building.** This imposing 1913 structure stands in 23ha (57 acres) of parkland and is a must-see for anyone interested in architecture, politics and history. South of the river is the **Muttart Conservatory** (1977), a dramatic addition to the Edmonton townscape. Housing a spectacular display of plants, its four glass pyramids have earned it the nickname "Giza on the Saskatchewan."

Don't miss a visit to the world's largest shopping and entertainment center, **West Edmonton Mall,** 15 minutes from downtown. In addition to more than 800 stores, attractions include Galaxyland, the world's largest indoor amusement park; World Waterpark, with swimming pools, slides, a wave pool and a bungee jump; and Deep Sea Derby, with bumper boats and water guns, Sea Lions' Rock, an interactive show, the Sea Life Caverns aquarium and Ice Palace skating rink.

www.edmonton.com

18K

Edmonton Tourism Gateway Park, 2404 Gateway Boulevard (Highway 2) 780/496-8400, 800/463/4667 (toll-free in North America)

Art Gallery of Alberta

Enterprise Square, 100-10230 Jasper Avenue 780/422-6223
Mon–Fri 10:30–5 (also 4–8pm Thu, free), Sat–Sun 11–5 Moderate

Alberta Legislative Building

98th Avenue and 107 Street 780/427-7362; www.assembly.ab.ca/visitor May to mid-Oct Mon–Fri 8:30–5, Sat–Sun 9–5 (tours hourly 9–12, every 30 mins 12:30–4); mid-Oct to Apr Mon–Fri 9–4:30 (tours hourly 9–3), Sat–Sun 12–5 (tours hourly 12–4) Free

Muttart Conservatory

9626–96A Street 780/496-8755; www.muttartconservatory.ca
Phone for details Moderate

West Edmonton Mall

8882 170 Street 780/444-5200; www.westedmall.com Mon–Sat 10–9, Sun 11–5 More than 100 dining options ($–$$$)

HEAD-SMASHED-IN BUFFALO JUMP

Head-Smashed-In is one of the best-preserved buffalo jumps in North America, designated a UNESCO World Heritage Site in 1981. For over 5,500 years the native people of the plains used it to kill the buffalo that provided them with food, hides for shelter and clothing, and bones and horns to make tools. A multimillion-dollar, five-level interpretive center, built into the cliff, tells the story of the Blackfoot people and their culture and lifestyle.

The buffalo would be panicked into a stampede then forced to follow a path that ended at a cliff. The animals simply ran off the edge and fell to their death, to be butchered in a camp at the base of the cliff. Only enough buffalo were killed to provide the tribe with what they actually needed. Below the cliff an accumulation of bones and ash from those times lies more than 9m (30ft) deep.

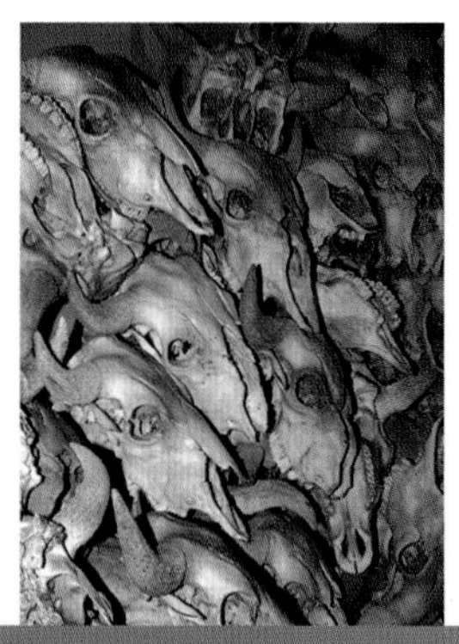

The site includes trails, viewpoints, dioramas, artifacts and an 80-seat theater that shows a short film recreating a buffalo hunt.
www.head-smashed-in.com

18L Highway 785 off Highway 2, 18 km (11 miles) northwest of Fort MacLeod, Alberta 403/553-2731 Mid-May to mid-Sep daily 9–6; mid-Sep to mid-May daily 10–5 Moderate Café ($)

LOWER FORT GARRY

The excellent Lower Fort Garry National Historic Park, 32km (20 miles) north of Winnipeg on Highway 9, contains North America's oldest intact stone fur-trading post, founded in 1881. Guides in period costume help visitors to experience life in the mid-1800s. You can talk to the "governor" and his wife up at the Big House, the heart of the complex, and listen to the staff describing their lives as they go about their daily tasks. All play their parts superbly. The visitor reception center shows a movie that gives a good introduction to the history of the fort, which was a key component in the Hudson's Bay Company network. There is also a small but exquisite collection of period artifacts, from First Nations household articles to imported porcelain. Other buildings include warehouses, a granary, a brewery, a sawmill and a well-stocked fur loft.

24L 5925 Highway 9, St. Andrews, Manitoba 888/773-8888; www.pc.gc.ca/lhn-nhs/mb/fortgarry Mid-May to early Sep daily 9–5; early Sep to mid-Oct daily 9–5, guided tours only at 11, 1 and 3 Moderate

MENNONITE HERITAGE VILLAGE

Around 65,000 Mennonites, members of a Protestant German-speaking sect, live in Manitoba. This authentic recreation of a typical Mennonite village occupies a site near Steinbach, 61km (38 miles) southeast of Winnipeg, and is a fascinating introduction to their culture and lifestyle from the 16th century to the present day. Among more than 30 traditional buildings are a windmill, a house-barn, a church, a schoolhouse and a semlin – a crude type of sod and wood house, built as a temporary shelter when the settlers first arrived. There's also a traditional outdoor clay oven where hearty breads and buns are baked. You can sample typical Mennonite fare in the Livery Barn Restaurant, and the general store sells Mennonite crafts, seeds, books and souvenirs.

www.mennoniteheritagevillage.com

24M Just north of Steinbach, on Highway 12, Manitoba 204/326-9661, 866/280-8741 (toll-free) Jul–Aug Mon–Sat 10–6, Sun noon–6; May–Jun, Sep Mon–Sat 10–5, Sun noon–5; Oct–Apr Mon–Fri 10–4 or by appointment Moderate Livery Barn Restaurant ($$, May–Sep)

REGINA

Regina grew from a small settlement called Pile o' Bones (after the buffalo bones left by First Nations hunters) into a cosmopolitan city and capital of Saskatchewan. It lies between Winnipeg and Calgary in the heart of Canada's "breadbasket."

The North West Mounted Police (later the Royal Canadian Mounted Police) established their headquarters here in the 1880s, and though this has since moved to Ottawa, the city has maintained its long association with the force through the training academy, where all Mounties learn their skills.

The **RCMP Heritage Centre,** previously the RCMP Museum, opened in 2007 in a new building that houses a series of exhibitions outlining the vivid history of the force and its modern and global role. You can also see the daily Sergeant Major's Drill

Parade at 12:45 and the Sunset Retreat Ceremony at 6:45pm, July to mid-August.

The small downtown area has little to offer visitors, but south of here is Wascana Park, the city's main recreation area, with a bandstand, barbecue pits, snack bars and boating and waterfowl ponds. This beautiful urban park is also home to the Saskatchewan Science Centre, the Conexus Arts Centre, the Royal Saskatchewan Museum, the Mackenzie Art Gallery and the Legislative Building, with its impressive dome.

21L

Tourism Regina PO Box 3355, Regina, Saskatchewan 306/789-5099, 800/661-5099; www.tourismregina.com

RCMP Heritage Centre

5907 Dewdney Avenue W 306/522-7333, 866/567-7267 (toll-free); www.rcmpheritagecentre.com Museum: mid-May to early Sep daily, 8–6:45; early Sep to mid-May 10–5 Moderate

RIDING MOUNTAIN NATIONAL PARK

Riding Mountain National Park rises dramatically from the surrounding prairie landscape and is part of the upland known as the Manitoba Escarpment. Its 2,966sq km (1,145sq miles) of rolling hills incorporate three very different landscapes – deciduous forest to the east, boreal forest to the north and aspen parkland in the west – and is home to a variety of wildlife, such as wolves, moose, elk, lynx, beavers, bears and bison.

Wasagaming, the main town, sits on Clear Lake, the largest body of water in the park. Its crystal waters are ideal for scuba diving, sailing and fishing for perch, pike and trout. With over 400km (250 miles) of trails and opportunities for downhill skiing at Agassiz Ski Hill, the park is a year-round playground. A visit to the First Nations Anishinabe Village gives a picture of life here before European settlement.

23L · Grey Goose Bus Lines (summer only) to Wasagaming · Moderate
Refreshments at Wasagaming and Lake Audy ($–$$)
Wasagaming, Manitoba · 204/848-7275; www.pc.gc.ca/riding
Visitor Centre: Jul–late Aug daily 9:30–8; late May–Jun, late Aug to mid-Oct daily 9:30–5:30

ROYAL TYRREL MUSEUM, DRUMHELLER

Best places to see, ➤ 52–53.

SASKATOON

Saskatoon was founded in 1883, though for some 8,000 years it had been inhabited by First Nations people. Their history can be explored at the **Wanuskewin Heritage Centre,** 5km (3 miles) north via Highway 11.

A small township developed here after the Canadian Pacific Railway brought settlers as far as Regina by rail, and railroad history is recalled at the **Saskatchewan Railway Museum.** The **Western Development Museum** has displays relating to the history of the province and the European settlement of the Prairies. This included a strong Ukrainian community, and the city is home to one of the country's premier collections of Ukrainian art and artifacts.

www.tourismsaskatoon.com

20K

Tourism Saskatoon 101–202 Fourth Avenue North, Saskatoon, Saskatchewan 306/242-1206, 800/567-2444

Wanuskewin Heritage Centre

Penner Road (RR4), 5km (3 miles) north of the city on Highway 11 306/931-6767; www.wanuskewin.com

Daily 9–5 Inexpensive

Saskatchewan Railway Museum

RR3 via highways 7 and 60 306/382-9855; www.saskrailmuseum.org Phone for details

Inexpensive

Western Development Museum

2610 Lorne Avenue 306/931-1910; www.wdm.ca

Apr–Dec daily 9–5; Jan–Mar Tue–Sun 9–5 Moderate

HOTELS

CALGARY, ALBERTA

Days Inn-Calgary Airport ($$)

This modern, small hotel has good comfortable rooms. The location is out of town, but there's an airport shuttle, and a ten-minute walk accesses the C-train light rail system direct to downtown. The hotel has a small pool.

2799 Sunridge Way 403/250-3297

Westin Calgary ($$$–$$$$)

Beautifully appointed rooms with modern decor and furnishings distinguish this hotel in a good downtown location. There are luxury suites also, and amenities include a rooftop pool, gym and restaurant.

320 4th Avenue 403/266-1611, 888/625-5144; www.westincalgary.com

DRUMHELLER, ALBERTA

Inn and Spa at Heartwood Manor ($$–$$$)

All the rooms are individually designed in this delightful old clapboard heritage building. The spa facilities are superb – ideal for those in need of some pampering.

320 North Railway Avenue E 403/823-6495, 888/823-6495 (toll-free); www.innsatheartwood.com

EDMONTON, ALBERTA

Union Bank Inn ($$$–$$$$)

A luxury hotel in the heart of downtown. The rooms are decorated in pastel shades and some bathrooms have jet tubs.

10053 Jasper Avenue 780/423-3600; www.unionbankinn.com

RESTAURANTS

CALGARY, ALBERTA

Earl's on Fourth ($–$$)

There are seven Earl's in Calgary. The menus are long and varied, and often include sophisticated dishes from around the world.

2401 4th Street SW 403/228-4141 Breakfast, lunch and dinner daily

River Café ($$–$$$)

More a restaurant than a café, this popular eating place stands in a park by the Bow River. The menu changes regularly and features such delights as organic beef tenderloin and roasted sablefish. Reservations essential.

Prince's Island Park 403/261-7670 Mon–Fri 11–3, daily 5–11 (10pm in winter), Sat–Sun brunch 10–3

Teatro ($–$$$)

Teatro is in a grandiose building at the heart of downtown. The inspiration for the food comes from northern Italy, but the cooking includes Far Eastern and West Coast (fish and seafood) influences.

Olympic Plaza, 200 8th Avenue SE 403/290-1012 Dinner daily, lunch Mon–Fri from 11:30am

EDMONTON, ALBERTA

The Creperie ($)

Traditional crêpes in a snug French eatery in downtown Edmonton. Vegetarian options plus such dishes as baked salmon and mussels Marseillaise.

10220 103rd Street 780/420-6656 Tue–Thu 11:30–9, Fri 11:30–11, Sat 5–10, Sun 5–9

REGINA, SASKATCHEWAN

Bushwakker Brewing Co Ltd ($)

See page 59.

Mediterranean Bistro ($)

This bistro, just off the TransCanada, has a wide selection of dishes, including chicken stuffed with spinach and feta and a delicious bouillabaisse.

2589 Quance Street E 306/ 757-1666 Daily 11–3, 5–11

SASKATOON, SASKATCHEWAN

John's ($$$)

Dark wood paneling and crisp white linen set the scene for an elegant meal in a central location. The menu includes superb

meat, fish and seafood dishes, including lobster and halibut.
✉ 401 21st Street E ☎ 306/244-6384 ⏲ Mon–Fri 11:30–11, Sat 4:30–11

WINNIPEG, MANITOBA

Beachcombers ($$)

See page 58.

Bistro 7 1/4 ($$–$$$)

The menu at this popular French-influenced restaurant includes delicious mussels in creative mayonnaise mixes, wild sockeye salmon, duck breast with honey roasted peaches, and garlic linguine with shrimp. It's a bit south of the center, but worth the trip.
✉ 725 Osborne Street South ☎ 204/777-2525 ⏲ Tue–Sat 11:30–10

SHOPPING

ANTIQUES

Antiques & Funk

Antiques and quirky collectibles at this large outlet.
✉ 474 Main Street, Winnipeg, Manitoba ☎ 204/943-4782

CLOTHES AND ACCESSORIES

Alberta Boot

See page 70.

Winnipeg Outfitters

Western wear and First Nations handicrafts. Cold-weather gear a specialty.
✉ 250 McPhillips Street, Winnipeg, Manitoba ☎ 204/775-9653

CRAFTS AND JEWELRY

Manitoba Museum Shop

Local arts and crafts highlighting the province's history and cultural heritage.
✉ 190 Rupert Avenue, Winnipeg, Manitoba ☎ 204/988-0615
⏲ Tue–Sun 11–4

FIRST NATIONS ART

Bayat Gallery

Inuit artists from Canada's Arctic showcase their work here.

✉ 163 Stafford Street, Winnipeg, Manitoba ☎ 204/475-5873

Northern Images

Highlights the work of Inuit and Dene artists.

✉ 2nd floor, Portage Place, Winnipeg, Manitoba ☎ 204/942-5501

MALLS

Eaton Center

Over 180 shops and services make this one of the busiest scenes at the heart of downtown Calgary, complete with its indoor garden. The complex is linked to Calgary's network of overhead walkways that connect numerous developments.

✉ 8th Avenue, Calgary, Alberta ☎ 403/441-4901

West Edmonton Mall

See pages 71, 73 and 159.

MARKETS

The Forks Market

Specialty foods, fresh produce and arts and crafts.

✉ One Forks Market Road, Winnipeg, Manitoba ☎ 204/942-6302

ENTERTAINMENT

NIGHTLIFE

Blush Ultra

Downtown Winnipeg's biggest club venue with huge dance space and four bars. In-house DJs and live bands keep things going.

✉ 323 Portage Avenue, Winnipeg, Manitoba ☎ 204/221-4583

Yardbird Suite

Great jazz from big-name performers.

✉ 11 Tommy Banks Way, Edmonton, Alberta ☎ 780/432-0428; www.yardbirdsuite.com 🕘 Mid-Sep to Jun Fri–Sat 9pm–1am. Jam session Tue

THEATERS AND PERFORMANCE

Centennial Concert Hall

Manitoba's premier performance facility with a varied program.
✉ 555 Main Street, Winnipeg, Manitoba ☎ 204/780-3333 (tickets); www.mbccc.ca 🕐 Year-round

Citadel Theatre

One of Canada's top live performing arts complexes.
✉ 9828 – 101A Avenue, Edmonton, Alberta ☎ 780/425-1820, 888/425-1820 (toll-free in Canada); www.citadeltheatre.com 🕐 Year-round

Conexus Arts Centre

The home of Opera Saskatchewan hosts all kinds of shows.
✉ 200A Lakeshore Drive ☎ 306/525-9999, 800/667-8497 (toll-free); www.conexusartscentre.ca 🕐 Year-round

Globe Theatre

Theater in the round by Saskatchewan's oldest company.
✉ 1801 Scarth Street, Regina, Saskatchewan ☎ 306/525-6400; www.globetheatrelive.com 🕐 Year-round

Manitoba Theatre Centre

Top performances in Canada's oldest English-language theater.
✉ 174 Market Avenue, Winnipeg, Manitoba ☎ 204/942-6537, 877/446-4500 (toll-free in Manitoba); www.mtc.mb.ca 🕐 Oct–May

MTS Centre

Massive sports and entertainment complex, hosting Manitoba Moose hockey games, ice shows, concerts and other events.
✉ Hargrave Street, Winnipeg, Manitoba ☎ 204/780-3333 (tickets); www.mtscentre.com

Southern Alberta Jubilee Auditorium

Home to the Calgary Opera and Alberta Ballet. Classical music, opera, drama and rock and pop concerts.
✉ 1415 14th Avenue Northwest, Calgary, Alberta ☎ 403/297-8000; www.jubileeauditorium.com/southern 🕐 Year-round

The North

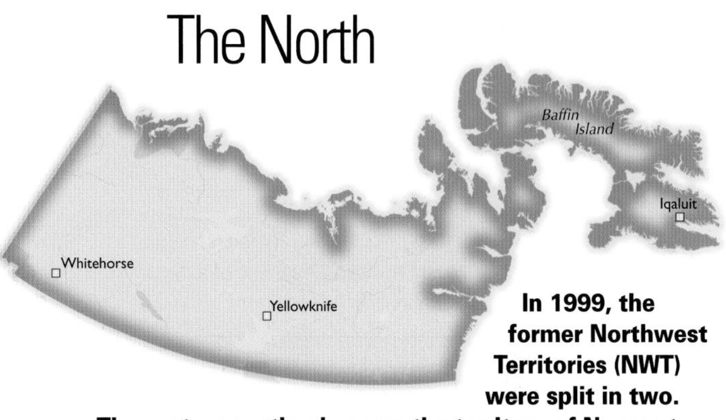

In 1999, the former Northwest Territories (NWT) were split in two. The eastern section became the territory of Nunavut (Inuit for "our land") and its capital (formerly Frobisher Bay) became Iqaluit. Covering almost a fifth of Canada, bounded to the south by Manitoba, it appears to be a frozen wasteland, but come spring it bursts into life and a beautiful patchwork of colorful flowers blankets the land. Together with the Yukon, these territories make up around 40 percent of Canada's land mass. Although the subarctic region has a handful of cities, nature dominates, and the area north of the Arctic Circle remains virtually uninhabited.

The Yukon will forever be associated with the Klondike Gold Rush, and the highways that cross it make it the easiest of the territories to get around. The NWT has fewer roads, but has two of the largest lakes in the world and is one of the world's last great wilderness refuges.

DAWSON CITY

Dawson City grew out of a marshy swamp near the confluence of the Klondike and Yukon rivers following the discovery of gold at Bonanza Creek in 1896. It became one of the most famous places on earth, but just three years later the rush came to an end and the prospectors were lured west to Alaska by news of a new strike at Nome, leaving Dawson to decline.

In 1953, the Yukon's first capital surrendered its role to Whitehorse, but a public campaign to preserve this important piece of Canada's history saw an upturn in Dawson's fortunes and today more than 30 buildings have been restored. Each summer the population swells as visitors come to sample the Dawson experience and soak up the atmosphere of days gone by, meandering the boardwalks and visiting national historic treasures; touring the Klondike Gold Fields and trying their luck panning for gold. The epicenters of the Gold Rush – Bonanza and Eldorado creeks – lie 19km (12 miles) from Dawson, and both make fascinating excursions.

www.dawsoncity.org

3B

Tourism Yukon Visitor Reception Centre and Klondike Visitors Association Corner of Front and King streets 867/993-5575 Mid-May to late Sep daily 8–8

Dawson City Museum

To place Dawson's restored buildings in their historical context pay a visit to the city museum, housed in a 1901 neoclassical building. Its three main galleries feature many exhibits on the Gold Rush era, including evocative photographs that highlight the difficult conditions in which the miners lived and worked, an early silent film that came to light in 1978 during a restoration project, and a reconstruction of the old Dawson City Courthouse.

Minto Park, next to the museum, has a collection of old locomotives and machinery from the Klondike's early mining days.
595 5th Avenue 867/993-5291; www.dawsonmuseum.ca Late May–Labour Day daily 10–6 Moderate Café ($)

Jack London Cabin and Interpretive Centre
Jack London came to the Klondike as a prospector in 1897, but like so many others he made no money. His experiences of life during those harsh days gave him plenty of material for the books he later wrote. He depicted the Yukon and Alaska as an enticing, rugged, unspoiled area in his novel *Call of the Wild.* His tiny cabin at Stewart Crossing, 120km (75 miles) south of town, has been re-created in Dawson City, and now contains an interpretive center illustrating his life, along with a small museum of memorabilia. Tours and readings of his works take place daily in summer.
8th Avenue, near Robert Service's Cabin 867/993-5575 Early May to mid-Sep daily 10–6 Inexpensive

Robert Service's Cabin
A walking tour of Dawson City takes you past the cabin of the English-born Canadian poet Robert Service (1874–1958). Here, the author of *The Shooting of Dan McGrew* and *The Cremation of Sam McGee*, which he wrote while living in Whitehorse, began full-time writing. The quaint little two-room cabin he rented contains its original woodstove, and stories and poetry recitals are offered daily in summer, along with tours of the site.
8th Avenue Mid-May to mid-Sep daily 9–noon and 1–5 Inexpensive

More to see in the North

ALASKA HIGHWAY

Starting at "Mile Zero" in Dawson Creek, the Alaska Highway makes its way northward through British Columbia and across the border with the Yukon. It's an exciting excursion into some of the wildest landscapes in the world. Watson Lake (Mile 635) is the first town in the Yukon and the location of the unusual Signpost Forest, started when a homesick soldier stuck up a sign pointing to his hometown of Denville, Illinois. Since then some 10,000 people have followed suit.

From here the Highway heads westward, dipping back into British Columbia before it reaches Teslin (Mile 804). After rounding the lake here it continues west again to Whitehorse (► 180–181; Mile 918). At this point, many travelers switch to the Klondike Highway (► 176–177) and continue to Haines Junction.

www.hellonorth.com

 4E

BAFFIN ISLAND

At just over 500,000sq km (193,000sq miles), Baffin is the largest island in the Canadian Arctic and the fifth largest in the world (sixth if you count Australia). It forms the major part of Nunavut, Canada's newest territory, and Iqaluit, formerly Frobisher Bay, is its capital. With a population of only 11,000 – mostly small Inuit groups – it is also one of the most sparsely populated areas in the world. Much of the island, a vast area of tundra, lies north of the Arctic Circle.

This far north the summer is very short and there are only a few hours of sunlight a day in winter. The big attraction is the Inuit lifestyle and culture, along with opportunities for wildlife spotting (polar bears, whales, walruses), outdoor activities such as hiking, kayaking, canoeing, dogsledding and snowmobiling, and the chance to see the aurora borealis (Northern Lights).

Baffin Island isn't the easiest of places to get to, or get around, but Iqaluit airport is a modern facility that also doubles as an alternative landing site for the U.S. space program. Several domestic Canadian airlines link the town with major Canadian centers. Just one highway links communities – the 26km (16-mile) route between Arctic Bay and Nanisivik on the Borden Peninsula in the far north.

A fly-in trip to the **Auyuittuq National Park** (21,760sq km/ 8,400sq miles) on the island's Cumberland Peninsula is a must. In the Inuit language, the name means "the land that never melts." Hiking and climbing are popular activities in June and July when the snow has melted and the meadows are covered with clumps of tundra grasses.

12B (off map) Flights to Iqaluit from Yellowknife, Ottawa and Montréal
Nunavut Tourism, Box 1450, Iqaluit, Nunavut 867/979-6551, 866/686-2888 (toll-free in North America); www.nunavuttourism.com

Auyuittuq National Park

PO Box 353, Pangnirtung, Nunavut 867/473-2500; www.pc.gc.ca/auyuittuq From Pangnirtung after ice melts in Jun

INUVIK AND THE MACKENZIE RIVER

Inuvik is the major settlement in the north of the Northwest Territories and makes an excellent base for exploring this vast Arctic region. It sits in the delta of the Mackenzie River, a wonderful freshwater environment. This lively town, with its multicolored homes raised above the permafrost, gives a cheerful splash of color to the otherwise barren wilderness. Look for the circular **Church of Our Lady of Victory** on the Mackenzie Road, a major landmark in the town. Painted white, it bears a striking resemblance to an igloo and is often referred to as the "igloo church." Inside you will find a series of paintings, *Stations of the Cross*, by local Inuit artist Mona Thresher. Each summer the town hosts the Great Northern Arts Festival, a ten-day gathering of artists and performers from across the Arctic and beyond.

You can charter a small plane to visit one of the national parks in the area – Ivvavik or Tuktut Nogait – where you can go hiking, kayaking and whitewater rafting, or view such wildlife as musk oxen, caribou and grizzly bears. In winter the chance to see the aurora borealis (Northern Lights) is a big draw. The Dempster Highway is the only road into Inuvik.

www.inuvik.ca

5A (Inuvik), 5A–7E (Mackenzie River) Twice-weekly Dawson City–Inuvik service Regular, from Yellowknife

Western Arctic Regional Visitor Centre, Mackenzie Road, Inuvik, Nunavut 867/777-4727 Jun–Sep

Church of Our Lady of Victory

174 Mackenzie Road 867/777-2236 Daily; tours available in summer

KLONDIKE HIGHWAY

The Klondike Highway follows the route taken by prospectors during the Gold Rush in the 1890s. Disembarking at Skagway in Alaska, U.S.A., they headed north on foot or horseback to

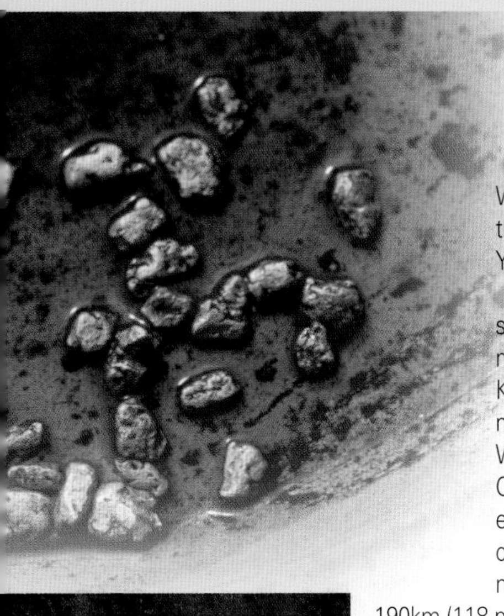

Whitehorse and continued their journey by boat on the Yukon River to Dawson City.

Technically the highway starts at Skagway, but for many people the real Klondike Highway is the northern section between Whitehorse and Dawson City. North of Whitehorse endless banks of conifers carpet the slopes of the mountains. Carmacks, 190km (118 miles) from Whitehorse, is a First Nations village named after George Carmacks, who first discovered gold in the area. About 22km (13.5 miles) farther you come to the halfway point at Five Fingers Rapids. The road then continues through Minto and Pelly Crossing to Stewart Crossing, location of Jack London's orginal cabin (➤ 173). The Silver Trail leads east from here, through the former silver mining towns of Mayo and Elsa to Keno, while the Klondike Highway continues to Dawson City, via Glenboyle. At Glenboyle the Dempster Highway heads northeast to Inuvik (➤ 176).

3C Daily bus Whitehorse to Dawson City (May–Sep) Vancouver, Calgary, Edmonton and Dawson City to Whitehorse

Tourist receptions at Whitehorse, Carmacks and Dawson City, Yukon

867/456-7623 for 24-hour information on the road; www.travelyukon.com

KLUANE NATIONAL PARK

Kluane National Park covers more than 22,000sq km (8,492sq miles) in the southwestern corner of the Yukon and takes its name from the Tutchone First Nations word meaning "place of many fish." This breathtaking park includes the mighty St. Elias Range, which contains the highest peak in Canada – Mount Logan (5,959m/19,551ft) – and the world's largest non-polar icefields, a vast network of more than 4,000 glaciers. Most of the park is inaccessible wilderness – the best way to see the icefields and the mountains is to take a tour in a small plane – but the Alaska Highway between Whitehorse and Beaver Creek will give you spectacular views of the distant mountains.

The main center, Haines Junction, is an obvious staging point for outdoor activities, with excellent opportunities for hiking. At the visitor center here you can find out everything you need to know about the park.

About 74km (46 miles) west of Haines Junction is Kluane Lake, a vast, beautiful stretch of glacier-fed water, 60km (37 miles) long, where you can rent a boat and fish for Arctic char and trout.

2C PO Box 5495, Haines Junction, Yukon
867/634-7250; www.pc.gc.ca/kluane
Expensive
Haines Junction Visitor Centre Mid-May to mid-Sep daily 9–5; by appointment rest of year
Tachal Dhal Visitor Centre Mid-May to mid-Sep daily 9–4

NAHANNI NATIONAL PARK

This unspoiled wilderness, in the southwest part of the NWT, is one of the most remote national parks in Canada. Within its boundaries is a section of the Mackenzie Mountains, with its high peaks, deep canyons, hot springs and waterfalls. The best way to see the park is to charter a small plane to Virginia Falls or Rabbitkettle Lake.

The spectacularly wild South Nahanni River is renowned as the world's premier whitewater rafting location, and Mount Wilson, at Moose Ponds, is a popular starting point for gentler canoe trips. Other highlights include the Tufa Mounds, 27m-high (88.5ft) domes of soft calcium; the Ragged Range, where molten igneous rock has been thrust up and eroded into jagged peaks; Rabbitkettle Hot Springs, where the water is a constant 20°C (68°F); and Virginia Falls, at 92m (300ft) twice the height of Niagara Falls, and with downstream canyons.

The park is home to many species of animals, including Dall's sheep, mountain goats, caribou and bears (black and grizzly). For very experienced mountaineers there is the Cirque of the Unclimbables, with its sheer rocky peaks.

5D

Nahanni National Park Reserve

Box 348, Fort Simpson, Northwest Territories

867/695-3151; www.pc.gc.ca/nahanni Park: daily. Office: mid-Jun to mid-Sep daily 8–12, 1–5; mid-Sep to mid-Jun Mon–Fri 8:30–12, 1–5

Expensive

WHITEHORSE

During the Gold Rush days of the 1890s, Whitehorse became an important town on the Klondike Highway from Skagway to Dawson City (➤ 172–173) as prospectors rested here before taking to the Yukon River for the last leg of their epic journey. The town really took off and developed when construction of the Alaska Highway (➤ 174) began in 1942, and it took over from Dawson City as capital of the Yukon in 1953. Today it is a lively town, and with the only major airport in the territory, it makes the perfect base for exploring the Yukon and the White Pass area. The **White Pass,** a steep, narrow ravine running southwest of Whitehorse to Skagway, Alaska, is one of the most dramatic routes in Canada and can be traveled by car or by the narrow-gauge railway.

Most people head first for the **SS *Klondike.*** This 1929 sternwheeler, now fully restored, used to travel the river between Whitehorse and Dawson City, carrying people and goods on the seven-day journey.

The **MacBride Museum,** in a charming log cabin on the scenic waterfront, gives a good account of the Yukon's past and Whitehorse's part in the Gold Rush, with a wonderful collection of photographs, archive material, Gold Rush memorabilia, and First Nations and Northwest Mounted Police exhibits. Outside are several reconstructed old buildings and a locomotive from the White Pass and Yukon Railroad.

West of Whitehorse are **Takhini Hot Springs,** where you can relax in an outdoor pool in natural mineral water maintained at a temperature of around 38°C (100.4°F).

3D From Calgary, Edmonton and Vancouver

Yukon Visitor Reception Centre 2121 2nd Avenue at Hanson Street, Whitehorse, Yukon 867/667-3084; www.city.whitehorse.yk.ca; www.visitwhitehorse.com

SS *Klondike*

Docked: 300 Main Street 800/661-0486 (toll-free); www.pc.gc.ca/ssklondike Mid-May to mid-Sep daily 9–6 Inexpensive

MacBride Museum

1124 - 1st Avenue 867/667-2709; www.macbridemuseum.com

Mid-May to Aug daily 9–6; Sep to mid-May Tue–Sat 12–4 Inexpensive

a drive around the Golden Circle

This spectacular drive passes through some of the most pristine landscape in North America, taking you across the border into Alaska, U.S.

Leave Whitehorse on 4th Avenue and Two Mile Hill to Route 1, the Alaska Highway (➤ 174), heading northwest to Haines Junction.

As you get close to Haines Junction, the mighty peaks of Kluane National Park (➤ 178) appear directly ahead.

After 160km (100 miles), at Haines Junction, take the Haines Highway south to Haines City.

Some 27km (17 miles) south of Haines Junction turn right to Kathleen Lake, a popular spot for hiking and camping.

Continue past Dezadeash Lake to Klukshu, a traditional First Nations autumn camp. Around 90km (56 miles) from Haines Junction you'll cross into British Columbia.

The views are dominated by the St. Elias Mountains to the right. The road leads to the Chilkat Pass (145km/90 miles), the highest on this highway at 1,065m (3,494ft).

After 178km (110.5 miles) you'll cross into Alaska, U.S.A. (customs post open 7am–11pm Alaska Time). Head 32km (20 miles) to the Chilkat Bald Eagle Preserve.

Thousands of eagles gather on the Chilkat Valley flats, especially in late autumn during the salmon spawning.

From here it's 35km (22 miles) to Haines City, a good place to stop overnight. Take the one-hour ferry ride from

Haines City to Skagway, a quaint "Gold Rush" town. Follow the Klondike Highway north out of town and up to White Pass, 22km (13.5 miles) away. It's another 11km (7 miles) to the customs post (in Canada).

North of Carcross is the Carcross Desert, the world's smallest at a little more than 1.6km (1 mile) long.

Where the Klondike Highway meets the Alaska Highway, it's 14km (8.5 miles) to Whitehorse.

Distance 483km (300 miles)
Time 2 days (not including time for hiking on park trails)
Start/end point Whitehorse 3D
Refreshment Antonio's Vineyard ($–$$) 202 Strickland Street, Whitehorse 867/668-6266; Raven Hotel ($$) Haines Junction 867/634-2500
Skagway Convention and Visitors Bureau 907/983-2854; www.skagway.com
Haines Convention and Visitors Bureau 907/766-2234; 800/458-3579 (toll-free); www.haines.ak.us
Warning: Distances between settlements are great. Keep an eye on your fuel at all times and plan ahead where you will stop for the night. Bring your passport and necessary documentation for the crossing into the U.S. Note: Alaska is one hour ahead of Pacific Standard Time.

YELLOWKNIFE

The capital of the Northwest Territories is the main base for exploring the north and the hub of many northern air routes. The heart of the city is the Old Town, along the shores of the Great Slave Lake, the perfect place for kayaking and canoeing or taking a summer cruise. Yellowknife is also a popular base for wildlife-viewing trips to see caribou and musk-ox herds, and for seeing the midnight sun and the aurora borealis (Northern Lights).

The town originated as a prospectors' camp that grew up when gold was found in the region is 1934, but it's famous now for diamonds. The Diavik Diamond Mines lie 320km (200 miles) northwest, but there's a visitor center in their Yellowknife office on 50th Avenue.

The area is the ancestral home of the Dogrib Dene First Nations. Their history is the focus of the excellent **Prince of Wales Heritage Centre,** off the Ingraham Trail, west of New Town. It's the principal museum for the region.

8E

Northern Frontier Visitor Centre

4807 49th Street 867/873-4262, 877/881-4642 (toll-free); www.discovernorth.ca

Mon–Fri 8:30–6 (till 5 Sep–May), Sat–Sun and hols 12–4

Prince of Wales Heritage Centre

4750 48th Street 867/873-7551; http://pwnhc.ca

Jun–Aug daily 10:30–5:30; Sep–May Mon–Fri 10:30–5, Sat–Sun 12–5 Free

Museum Café ($–$$; Mon–Fri 11:30–4)

HOTELS

DAWSON CITY, YUKON

Westmark Inn ($–$$)

Spacious, comfortable complex renowned for its Klondike barbecues. Some of the modern rooms and suites have kitchens.

5th and Harper streets 867/993-5542; www.westmarkhotels.com
Closed Oct–Apr

WHITEHORSE, NORTHWEST TERRITORIES

High Country Inn ($$)

This friendly place – with its huge wooden cut-out of a Mountie – has reasonable rooms and service. Facilities include a complimentary airport shuttle and an exercise room.

4051 4th Avenue 867/667-4471, 800/554-4471 (toll-free); www.highcountryinn.yk.ca

YELLOWKNIFE, NORTHWEST TERRITORIES

Chataeu Nova ($$)

Everything is modern at this downtown hotel, including a fitness room with hot tub, and high-speed internet access in all 80 rooms.

4401 50th Avenue 877/839-1236 (toll-free); www.chateaunova.com

RESTAURANTS

DAWSON CITY, YUKON

Klondike Kate's ($)

Canadian and ethnic-influenced food served in an old original Gold Rush building. Good vegetarian options. Great breakfasts.

3rd Avenue and King Street 867/993-6527; www.klondikekates.ca
Apr–Sep daily 6:30am–11pm

WHITEHORSE, YUKON

Talisman ($)

First Nations owned and operated, this is a friendly place with good home-style cooking. The portions are generous and there's a wide choice of breakfast options.

River View Hotel, 102 Wood Street 867/667-7801 Summer Mon–Sat 7am–8pm, Sun 8–4; winter Mon–Sat 8–4 (to 7 Thu and Fri), Sun 8–2

YELLOWKNIFE, NORTHWEST TERRITORIES

L'Heritage Restaurant Francais ($$$)

Elegant French cuisine and a menu heavily influenced by regional ingredients is part of the experience at this gem of a restaurant. There's also an informal bistro downstairs.

5019 - 49th Street 867/873-9561 Mon–Sat 5–10pm

SHOPPING

ARTS AND CRAFTS

Midnight Sun Gallery and Gifts

Local arts and crafts, including jewelry, posters and pottery.

205C Main Street, Whitehorse, Yukon 867/668-4350;

CLOTHES AND ACCESSORIES

Wolverine Sports Shop

An excellent range of outdoor wear and camping gear.

Stantons Plaza, 100 Borden Drive, Yellowknife, NWT 867/873-4350

ENTERTAINMENT

Diamond Tooth Gertie's Gambling Hall

A Gold Rush-style saloon; Canada's oldest casino.

Queen Street 867/993-5525, Dawson City, Yukon Early May–Sep Sun–Wed 7pm–2am, Fri–Sat 2pm–2am; some winter opening – call for information Cover charge: moderate

Frantic Follies

A turn-of-the-20th-century vaudeville revue.

Westmark Whitehorse Hotel, 2nd Avenue and Wood Street, Whitehorse, Yukon 867/668-2042; www.franticfollies.com Late May to early Sep

Yukon Arts Centre

One of the few cultural venues in the vast and empty North. Regularly hosts world-class performers, international dance and theater companies, as well as classical recitals and concerts.

300 College Drive, Whitehorse, Yukon 867/667-8484 (and press 2); www.yukonartscentre.com Year-round

Sight Locator Index

This index relates to the maps on the covers. We have given map references to the main sights of interest in the book. Grid references in italics indicate sights featured on the town plan. Some sights within towns may not be plotted on the maps.

Index

Acknowledgments

The Automobile Association wishes to thank the following photographers, companies and picture libraries for their assistance in the preparation of this book. Abbreviations for the picture credits are as follows – (t) top; (b) bottom; (l) left; (r) right; (c) centre; (AA) AA World Travel Library

4l Yoho NP, AA/P Bennett; **4c** Icefields Parkway, Banff, AA/P Bennett; **4r** Sulphur Mountain, Banff, AA/P Timmermans; **5l** Icefields Parkway, AA/C Sawyer; **5c** Granville Island, Vancouver, AA/C Sawyer; **6/7** Yoho NP, AA/P Bennett; **8/9** Vancouver, AA/C Sawyer; **10/11** Jasper NP, AA/C Sawyer; **10ct** Mountie, AA/C Coe; **10cb** Calgary, Saddledome, AA/P Bennett; **10b** Maple leaf symbol, AA/C Coe; **11ct** Glenbow Museum, Calgary, AA/C Sawyer; **11cb** Aspen forest, Bow Valley Parkway, AA/P Bennett; **11b** Whale, AA; **12/13t** Salmon for sale, AA/M Dent; **12c** Restaurant in Calgary, AA/P Bennett; **13b** Fishermen, AA/J-F Pin; **13t** Cowichan Vallery Winery, AA/P Bennett; **13b** Steak, AA/P Bennett; **14t** Vancouver's Raintree Restaurant, AA/M Dent; **14c** Wine bottles, AA/C Coe; **14/15** Stevenston Fish Market, Vancouver, AA/M Dent; **15** Beer bottles, AA/J-F Pin; **16/17** Horsehouse Canyon, Drumheller Badlands, AA/P Bennett; **16** Badlands, Dinosaur Prov Park, AA/P Bennett; **17** Wheat, AA/C Coe; **18t** Moraine Lake, AA/C Sawyer; **18/19** Pacific Rim NP, AA/C Sawyer; **19t** Grizzly Bear, AA/P Bennett; **19b** Dawson City General Store, AA/P Bennett; **20/21** Icefields Parkway, Banff, AA/P Bennett; **25** Calgary Stampede, Paolo Koch/Robert Harding; **27** Cirrus Mountain, Banff NP, AA/P Bennett; **28** Air Canada aircraft, AA/P Bennett; **28/29** Burrard Inlet, AA/P Bennett; **34/35** Sulphur Mountain, Banff, AA/P Timmermans; **36** Moraine Lake, Banff NP, AA/P Bennett; **36/37** Vermillion Lake, AA/C Sawyer; **37** Aspen Forest, Bow Valley Parkway, AA/P Bennett; **38/39** Butchart Gardens, AA/H Harris; **38** Butchart Gardens, AA/C Sawyer; **40/41** Horseshoe Bay, AA/P Timmermans; **41** Howe Sound, AA/C Coe; **42** Kluane NP, AA/C Coe; **43** Icefields Parkway, AA/C Sawyer; **44/45** Maligne Lake, AA/C Sawyer; **45** Horseriders, AA/C Sawyer; **46, 47** Museum of Manitoba, Winnipeg, AA/P Bennett; **48** Museum of Anthropology, Vancouver, AA/C Coe; **49tl, 49b** Museum of Anthropology, Vancouver, AA/P Bennett; **49tr** Museum of Anthropology, Vancouver, AA/C Sawyer; **50** Emerald Lake, Yoho NP, AA/C Sawyer; **50/51** Moraine Lake, AA/P Bennett; **52** Royal Tyrell Museum, Drumheller, AA/P Bennett; **52/53** Royal Tyrell Museum, Drumheller, AA/P Bennett; **53** Royal Tyrell Museum, Drumheller, AA/C Sawyer; **54/55** Stanley Park, Vancouver, AA/C Sawyer; **56/57** Icefields Parkway, AA/C Sawyer; **58/59** Blackcomb Mountain, restaurant, AA/P Bennett; **60** Jasper, men on horseback, AA/C Sawyer; **61** Blackcomb Mountains, skiers, AA/P Bennett; **62** Mount Bourgeau, Banff NP, AA/P Bennett; **63** Dawson City, panning for gold, AA/C Coe; **64/65** Emerald Lake, Yoho NP, AA/J Tims; **66** Emerald Lake, Yoho NP, AA/P Bennett; **67** Peyto Lake, AA/P Bennett; **69** Canada Place, Vancouver, AA/C Coe; **70/71** Metro Town Mall, Vancouver, AA/P Bennett; **73** Vancouver, Playland, AA/M Dent; **74/75** Granville Island, Vancouver, AA/C Sawyer; **77** Alaska Highway, AA/C Coe; **78** Canada Place, Vancouver, AA/P Timmermans; **79** Canada Place, Vancouver, AA/P Bennett; **80t** Chinatown, Vancouver, AA/P Bennett; **80b** Chinatown, Vancouver, AA; **80/81** Granville Island, Vancouver, AA/C Sawyer; **82** Maritime Museum, Vancover, AA/C Sawyer; **82/83** Grouse Mountain, view to Vancouver, AA/P Bennett; **84** Geodesic Dome, Vancouver, AA/P Timmermans; **84/85** Stanley Park Aquarium, Vancouver, AA/C Sawyer; **86/87** Stanley Park Aquarium, Vancouver, AA/C Sawyer; **86** Vancouver Art Gallery, AA/P Timmermans; **88t** Alaska Highway, AA/C Coe; **88b** Alaska Highway roadsign, AA/P Bennett; **89** Alaska Highway, AA/C Coe; **90t** Banff town centre, AA/P Bennett; **90b** Banff Springs Hotel, AA/C Sawyer; **91** Goldrush Trail sign, AA/P Bennett; **92** Fraser River, AA/M Dent; **93** Monashee Mountains, AA/P Bennett; **94** Jasper, AA/C Coe; **94/95** Kootenay Lake, AA/OTB; **95** Kootenay Hot Springs, AA/C Coe; **96** Lake Louise, Hikers, AA/P Bennett; **97** View towards Lake Louise, AA/P Bennett; **98** Lake Louise, AA/C Coe; **98/99** Lake Osoyoos, AA/P Timmermans; **100** Buffalo Herd, Waterton Lakes NP, AA/P Bennett; **100/101** Buffalo Herd, Waterton Lakes NP, AA/P Bennett; **101** Helmecken Falls, Wells Gray Prov Park, AA/C Sawyer; **103** Icefields Parkway, AA/C Sawyer; **104t** Whistler, chairlift, AA/P Bennett; **104b** Whistler town, AA/P Bennett; **113** Port Alberni, Pacific Rim NP, AA/C Sawyer; **114** Empress Hotel, Victoria, AA/C Sawyer; **116/117** Inner Harbour, Victoria, AA/C Sawyer; **117** Maritime Museum, Victoria, AA/C Sawyer; **118** Parliament Buildings, Victoria, AA/C Sawyer; **119** Royal British Columbia Museum, Victoria, AA/M Dent; **121** Shops, Victoria, AA/P Bennett; **122/123** Cathedral Grove, AA/P Bennett; **123** Shops, Chamainus, AA/P Bennett; **124/125t** Nanaimo, AA/P Bennett; **124/125b** Long Beach, Pacific Rim NP, AA/C Coe; **126** Wood, Prince Ruper, AA/C Coe; **128** Grey Whale, AA/P Bennett; **135** Riding Mountain NP, AA/P Bennett; **136** Legislature Building, Winnipeg, AA/P Bennett; **138/139** Downtown Winnipeg, AA/P Bennett; **139** Exchange District, Winnipeg, AA/P Bennett; **140/141** The Forks Area, Winnipeg, AA/P Bennett' **141t, b** Winnipeg Art Gallery; **142/143** Legislature Building, Winnipeg, AA/P Bennett; **144/145** Calgary Skyline, AA/C Coe; **145** Calgary Tower, AA/C Coe; **146t** Calgary Zoo, AA/P Bennett; **146c, b** Calgary Zoo, AA/P Bennett; **147t** Fort Calgary, AA/P Bennett; **147b** Fort Calgary, AA/C Sawyer; **148t, b** Glenbow Museum, Calgary, AA/C Sawyer; **150, 150/151** Batoche National Historical Site, AA/P Bennett; **151** Remington Carriage Museum, Cardston, AA/P Bennett; **152/153** Loch Leven, Cypress Hills Prov Park, AA/P Bennett; **153t** Cypress Hills Prov Park, AA/P Bennett; **153b** Fort Walsh, Cypress Hills Prov Park, AA/P Bennett; **155** Cypress Hills Prov Park, AA/P Bennett; **156** Dinosaur Prov Park, Alberta Badlands, AA/P Bennett; **156/157** Horseshoe Canyon, AA/P Bennett; **158t** Edmonton, AA/P Bennett; **158r** Edmonton, Muttart Conservatory, AA/P Bennett; **159** World Waterpark, Edmonton, AA/P Bennett; **160t** Head Smashed in Buffalo Jump, AA/P Bennett; **160b** Head Smashed in Buffalo Jump, AA/P Bennett; **161** Lower Fort Garry, AA/P Bennett; **162/163** Regina, AA/P Bennett; **163** Legislative Building, Regina, AA/P Bennett; **164** Riding Mountain NP, AA/P Bennett; **164/165** Saskatoon, Wanuskewin Heritage Park, AA/P Bennett; **165** Saskatoon, Wanuskewin Heritage park, AA/P Bennett; **171** Alaska Highway, AA/C Coe; **172/173** Robert Service Cabin, Dawson, AA/C Coe; **174** Alaska Highway, AA/C Coe; **176** Dawson, building, AA/C Coe; **176/177** Gold nuggets, Dawson, AA/C Coe; **177** Dawson, gold mining equipment, AA/C Coe; **178/179** Kluane Lake, AA/C Coe; **180/181** Carcross Hotel, AA/C Coe; **181t** Whitehorse, log skyscraper, AA/P Bennett; **181b** SS Klondike, Whitehorse, AA/C Coe; **183** St Elias Mountains, AA/C Coe; **184** Kluane Lake, AA/C Coe

Every effort has been made to trace the copyright holders, and we apologise in advance for any unintentional omissions or errors. We would be pleased to apply any corrections in any following edition of this publication.